Through the
Ganesh Gate

by Melanie Serpa

For information regarding permission, visit www.SquigglyLineMedia.com.

For information on the author, visit www.MelanieSerpa.com.

ISBN-13: 978-0-9841289-5-2   ISBN-10: 0-9841289-5-6

Published by Squiggly Line Media, Portland, Oregon USA.

Printed in the USA - First printing, February 2016

Squiggly Line
M E D I A ™

To Zane

To Loretta –
Happy Reading!

Melanie [signature]

One

The passport slipped from Maddy's fingers and her world blurred for a moment. The crisp, blank pages fluttered for an instant before they collided with the cold tile floor. She stood at her kitchen counter staring down at it. The passport was new, stiff and formal; the gold eagle embossed in profile. She lifted herself, pressed her palms to her forehead and leaned into her hands with a groan. What had she gotten herself into? She was not a world traveler, or any kind of traveler for that matter. Why had she agreed to this trip?

And then there was Richard. They barely got along at home even with all the built-in distractions. How were they going to travel together without killing one another? Maddy felt a sickening panic rise in her chest like a kettle nearing a boil. She wanted to scream, to run, but as always, she took a deep breath to slow her racing heart. She wiped her watering eyes and picked up the passport again. She would find a way to get through this. Maybe she would even enjoy seeing the world. If she could make it to Nepal, she could walk and walk for days. She would just have to hold it together until then; everything will be alright, she muttered.

Before bed, Maddy showered and combed out her long brown hair. As she passed the mirror, she caught a glimpse of her body. The reflection bounced between the full length mirror and the smaller vanity. Droplets of water glistened on her skin in the soft bathroom light. She marveled at the pliability of the human body, its capacity to shift and morph over time and circumstance. Nearly thirty, she was beginning to see the tiny changes that came with life and age; a bit more cellulite, a little less spring in the skin. Especially since the baby. She forced that memory away, back into its dark compartment, and shifted her eyes down. Hiking all spring had helped tone her legs in preparation for trekking. Day hikes at Mt. Bachelor had provided the hours and elevation required for breaking in her new boots and carrying a pack. Maddy looked at her narrow shoulders and hoped they were strong enough to lift her travel pack in the days to come. A ripple of fear ran through her belly and she turned away from the mirror. She tried to focus on the trip, the adventure, not her fear, and definitely not Richard.

Maddy slipped into bed and lay in the darkness. She listened as Richard came in and dropped his keys on the dresser. He stepped over the backpacks, eased open the closet door, and put his clothes in the hamper. He made a fair attempt to be quiet, but it didn't matter, she was not asleep. In an effort to appear so, she breathed deep and slow. These days, she tried to go to bed before Richard got home, to avoid an argument. Given how late he usually arrived, he was likely avoiding her in kind. Richard took a short shower and brushed his teeth in the hot spray.

Despite her efforts, Maddy felt a chill and her muscles tensed as Richard slid into bed. His long frame did not touch her, but his body was so close she could feel the heat from the shower. Richard's breath, shallow at first, dropped deeper and deeper as he sank into sleep. Maddy turned away, her mind going through endless packing lists in a vain attempt to mask her fear of flying and the dread she felt about traveling with a husband she hardly knew anymore. She breathed like a scuba diver conserving precious air. Each breath became so slow and forced that she would either fall asleep, or pass out from hypoxia. Either would have been fine with her.

The thunk of the newspaper landing on the doorstep woke her at six AM. She'd had a paper route growing up but had delivered the papers in the afternoon after school in time to read with diner. Now, the paper came early, sometimes before dawn, delivered not by kids earning spending money but by underemployed adults making ends meet. Rolling over, she found Richard's side of the bed empty. He had likely gone out for a last round of golf with his buddies before they left tomorrow.

The house seemed foreign, personality-less with all the pictures packed away. A friend of a friend would be

3

coming to live there while they were away and so only the big furniture had been left out. The rest of their belongings had been boxed and squirreled away to the attic. Maddy retrieved the paper and opened it on the counter. The Bend Bulletin announced that Hong Kong had returned to Chinese rule and that in Cambodia, the Khmer Rouge was set to hold trial for former leader Pol Pot for his war crimes. 1997 was sure to be an interesting year for international events, Maddy thought.

She wondered what news would look like from the other side of the world. Newspapers were likely to be her main source of information as hostels and guesthouses may not have televisions. A nervous butterfly flitted through her stomach. She hoped she could handle a year of travel; being away from a routine, from all that was known and comfortable. She would try her best to travel well. She took a deep breath to push away the fear and went upstairs to finish her final packing.

Two

The mammoth engine roared to life beneath the Boeing 777 and bumped away from the gate. Jammed between Richard and a burly man who took up part of her seat, Maddy was nearly hyperventilating and white-knuckling the armrests. She hated take-offs and landings; actually, she hated to fly. Maddy rifled through the seat pouch in front of her to find the safety card. She read it twice, especially memorizing what to do in the event of a water landing. It was ridiculous, she knew, since no plane ever "landed" on water. She found the air sick bag and said a prayer, then turned her attention to the Virgin Atlantic courtesy bag. Maddy gently pulled each item from the small bag. First, she inserted the squishy red earplugs and felt relieved as the rustling of Richard's newspaper receded. Next, she found the soft red and white striped socks that looked straight out of The Cat in the Hat. The last little goody was an eye mask with the word, "Virgin" printed across the front. The title was apropos. She felt like a virgin traveler: first time on an international flight; first time flying over water; first major leg of this journey into the world.

A gentle tap made Maddy jump. She peeked out from

under her eye mask.

"Ello darling." The flight attendant chirped. "Would you like a sweet?" She held out a white Virgin bowl filled with red and purple pinwheel mints.

"Thank you." Maddy said taking one, then retreating back under the eye mask to practice some deep breathing. The pilot announced they were cleared for takeoff and the flight attendants were seated. The plane bumped again and Maddy felt tears well up beneath her mask. She was quiet at first, snuffling into a bandana she'd pulled from her bag. As the plane taxied, hovered, then rose into the air pulling Maddy deep into her seat, panic consumed her. Despite efforts to the contrary, she cried in tune with the whine of the engines and gasped as the plane banked left on its course. The mask, now sopping, was glued to her face. In her personal darkness, she was oblivious to the other passenger's stares and raised eyebrows as her anxiety climbed.

She had not always been this way. When she'd traveled for work, flying had become as mundane as riding the bus. But one flight years ago had sparked the fear that now enveloped her. She had been flying from Seattle to Philadelphia to check out a hospital for a potential job. Storms had ravaged the West, then plodded east the week before. Her hope was that the foul weather would clear the East Coast before she arrived, but a band of storms stalled and held in place.

An hour out of Philly, the pilot announced that they

would be delayed due to ice on the runway, and that flight control was considering a different airport. The flight attendants collected trash and buckled up ready for instruction. Thunder and lightning surrounded the airplane and turbulence buffeted the wings as they entered the storm. The plane bucked wildly, dipped and dodged. Passengers cried out like a bell chorus throughout the metal cabin. The plane was tossed about the sky like a beach ball. Maddy was caught up in the rising panic and she watched the flight attendants huddle and talk about the emergency procedures.

The pilot, in a firm and concerned voice, announced that there were no other options and they were going to land in Philadelphia. Because of the freezing rain, the pilot said they would have to descend rapidly. Maddy overheard people discussing the physics of freezing rain just as the plane pointed nose down and hurtled toward the airport. The descent, usually done gradually over half an hour, took just a few minutes. All the passengers, herself included, screamed as the plane careened downward. Maddy had squeezed her eyes shut, choosing darkness over the carnage that was surely coming. The man next to her placed the oxygen mask over her face when she failed to do so.

Moments before the runway, Maddy felt her body suck into the seat as the plane pulled up abruptly. It jerked to level, and touched down on a solid sheet of ice. In a slow motion ballet, the plane skidded and pirouetted. Maddy opened her eyes just to in time to watch the runway lights twirl by on the second spin. At the very end of the runway, the plane tipped off onto the adjacent grass. It rested slightly forward onto its nose due to the collapse of the front wheels. An awkward silence was followed by passengers erupting in shouts and cheers of relief. Maddy sat immobilized, shivering, and clutching the armrests.

Richard looked over at Maddy and rolled his eyes. "You had better get ahold of yourself, this is just the beginning," he said. Embarrassment oozed from his curt tone. He turned back toward the window and resumed reading his paper.

She waited for the flight to smooth out but it did not. The fasten-seatbelt sign remained illuminated long after they had achieved cruising altitude because the plane would not stop bouncing and jerking. Maddy reminded herself that she had survived before, and this flight would be fine. But her body remembered the terror; so much for the hypnosis. When the pilot announced that they were flying above Nova Scotia, Maddy realized they were out over open water. Once again, her sobs filled the cabin and each flight attendant came by in turn to calm her. One brought a box of Kleenex, the next offered the bowl of sweets. The third offered a drink as did the fourth; Richard accepted both. Maddy sat hunched in her misery until a tall red skirted attendant stopped and took her hand.

"Come with me," the attendant said, and gently pulled Maddy out of her seat and led her to the back of the cabin.

"Take a Xanax." Richard called as they walked down the aisle. The plane jostled and rattled with every step.

Maddy, with red swollen eyes and hair disheveled by the Virgin mask, followed the woman without question. After all the fuss Maddy had made, she would not have been surprised if the attendant had stuffed her purple scarf in Maddy's mouth and locked her in the bathroom. Instead, a slender hand motioned to a small harnessed seat in the galley.

"Sit here with us." The beautiful attendant smiled graciously as Maddy buckled into the weensy jump seat and was handed a plastic cup of sparkling water. The bubbles leapt and popped above the rim; she held it close to her face to feel the tiny spray.

The flight never smoothed out but Maddy found comfort in the quiet chatter of calm British accents talking about daily events. They seemed not to notice the bumpy ride over the Atlantic. They had likely logged a million miles among them and seemed immune to the visceral weightlessness of thirty-eight thousand feet. Slightly stoned now that the Xanax had kicked in, Maddy was guided back to her seat and passed out for the remainder of the flight. She woke as the flight attendants were clearing away the trash before descent. Despite her fear, the landing was textbook. Maddy hugged each perfectly primped flight attendant as she went off the plane then bent to touch the ground, grateful to feel solid earth under her feet.

It took two baguettes slathered with mountains of butter and a stingy cappuccino for Maddy to metabolize all the Xanax and to get her brain organized around the fact that she was sitting in Paris. Chairs and miniature bistro tables sat facing the street outside the Parisian café. She noticed that people eating inside sat facing each other, but outside, patrons faced the street. Perfect, she thought; Maddy and Richard could share a table but not have to face one another. Why hadn't she thought of this simple solution at home?

Women in stylish leather boots, slim jeans tucked inside, wore scarves tied causally about their necks. Parisian fashion looked easy and yet sophisticated. No one wore shorts or sweat pants. Every person looked fit and put together. Maddy looked down at her frumpy, already wrinkled shapeless dress. She would have to get used to wearing one of the five outfits she had packed. None were stylish, just practical.

"What are you looking at?" Richard asked.

"I'm just noticing how no one on the street is disheveled, or overweight, or wearing sweats. They all look so stylish, unlike us," Maddy said glancing at Richard's Teva sandals.

"You worry too much," Richard said.

"It was just an observation. Americans seem to go out wearing anything, even pajamas," Maddy said.

"You're also judgmental," Richard said and drained his coffee cup.

Maddy shrugged and tried to ignore his criticisms. She felt a quick urge to toss her cup at him. Instead, she buried her face in the map and tried to find the Louvre. She still couldn't believe she was in Paris. She had dreamed of being in the iconic city for years but never thought that she would make it over the ocean.

They walked past the Eiffel Tower and around the Champs Elysees. Maddy's heart pounded with excitement as they walked toward the Louvre. This famous museum seemed straight out of a fairy tale. But as she approached, she squinted at the panes of glass. The glass pyramid in the center of the entry courtyard did not match the stone architecture of the main building. Built in 1989, the incongruent glass structure served as the main entrance to the museum. Maddy scanned the exterior of the older sections of building, which looked more like a u-shaped palace wrapped around a huge grass courtyard.

"How odd that glass looks," Maddy said, but Richard was out of earshot. He loitered near the green expanse of lawn that bordered the brick walkway.

"I can't believe we're here," Maddy called. "Let's go in."

"How long do you plan to stay?" Richard asked.

"I don't know. I want to see as much as I can." Maddy wondered what was up.

"Well, I've been here before." Richard shrugged. "I'm

going to the café for a while. You come find me when you're done."

What in the world? This trip was his idea. Now he was going to just sit in the café? She was relieved and angry all at once. She could see the amazing art without having Richard pestering or criticizing her. But a small part of her was disappointed. Did she think that seeing the Louvre together could heal their rift?

Maddy turned and shouted, "Well, I'm going in." She disappeared into the glass structure, down the escalator. A small burning ball sat in her stomach as she cued up for a ticket. Still breathing heavily, Maddy stepped up to the counter. She must have had a scowling look on her face because the petite woman behind the counter gave her a strange look. Maddy lowered her eyes.

"Is a ticket required for the café?" Maddy asked.

The Parisian cashier looked like she had just sucked on a lemon. "Oui Madame." She said and handed Maddy two tickets.

Maddy found Richard along the back wall and handed him one. "Apparently the café is full of art too," Maddy said.

She unfolded the huge map supplied by the cashier and scanned the floor plans. Exhibit halls stacked up in a blocky U-shape, with the underground floors also having a grand central gallery.

"Oh crap," Maddy said turning the map over, hoping for a different version on the back. "Everything is in French."

There was not an English title to be found. Additionally, the descriptions of the collections were also in French.

Richard smirked. "Have fun with that. See you later."

Maddy decided to start at the bottom and work her way up. Each floor offered up room after room of paintings, artifacts, and sculptures from the modern to the ancient. Maddy overheard an English-speaking docent explain that the building was originally constructed as a fortress in the 12th century under Phillip II. Several rulers since then had expanded the museum in order to add to their royal collections.

She wandered past a giant Sphinx into the Egyptian Antiquities. Given the age of the pieces, it was remarkable that they were so intact. Sarcophagi lined one wall and displayed classic ornamentation of Egyptian symbols. She strolled between stone tablets and marveled at the hieroglyphic writing, wondering what stories were embedded in the script. Maddy peered at the largest mummy laid out in an ornate sarcophagus. The petrified face was broad, male, and the color of dusty copper. Amazingly intact white teeth protruded in a tight row, leathery skin pulled back against cheek bones. Maddy's eyes went fuzzy for a moment and she felt suddenly hot. She pressed her head against the cool glass for support. The mummy morphed before her eyes. It was still stone-like, but now the face was familiar. She pressed her nose hard against the glass and realized the dead remains looked just like Richard. The body was bound in the tight cloth wrappings, but the face was definitely his. She looked away and shook her head, catching her reflection in the glass. A broad smile had replaced her typical furrowed brow. Maddy stepped back from the exhibit and looked around to see if anyone had noticed her wicked grin. Tourists milled around but paid her no mind. She buried her face in the all-French map and left the Egyptian display.

Maddy visited the impressionists' paintings and the work from the Renaissance era. She covered each floor of the massive museum working her way toward the top. By late afternoon she found Richard who had not budged from the café. Six empty wine glasses lined up like soldiers amid a landscape of bread crumbs and smeared butter.

"Hey Maddy," he slurred as she approached. It came out more like 'Marty.' He waved a limp hand at her.

Her heart sank. Of course. She should have known that they would serve alcohol in a Paris museum. She sat down in the empty chair next to him. He had never wanted to see the Louvre with her, he had known that he could drink all day and be away from her. This was yet another false prospect. He had been a non-drinker when they met in college, which was a nice change from Maddy's perspective. She had dealt with years of hassle growing up in a tiny town where the drinking age was eighteen and everyone started long before that. She had always been the designated driver, the one to clean up the mess, the one to bail her friends out of jail. Meeting Richard, who did not drink at the time, was a wonderful treat and surprise. Until her wedding night.

Maddy had enjoyed their casual outdoor ceremony and was pleased that so many of their friends had made the trip to the Olympic Peninsula for the wedding. Music blared from live guitars and filled the warm night air with rhythm and laughter. Richard, caught up in the festive atmosphere, decided it would be fun to have just one drink. One was followed by two, then three, four, and five.

Twice Maddy asked the band to wrap up before it was too late, but years of abstinence had lowered Richard's tolerance for alcohol. By eleven o'clock, he was smashed; by midnight, he couldn't walk. After an angry confrontation with Maddy, the groomsmen ladled Richard into bed, where he passed out cold. Since that night, Richard drank; anything and everything.

"Have you seen it all?" Richard asked of the museum.

"Almost. I want to see the Mona Lisa before we go," Maddy said.

"I'll come with you." Richard slid off the stylish stool and pushed a handful of Euro across the bar. Maddy winced; the bills were the equivalent to two days travel budget in Nepal.

"Mona Lisa, Mona Lisa," Richard sang. Maddy stepped away as he staggered toward her. To refocus her mind, she recalled the vision of his mummified corpse. It wouldn't be so far-fetched, she thought, he was already pickled on the inside.

"What a curious face," said a bedazzled Australian

woman who stood before the Mona Lisa. Maddy stared as well. It was true what people had said, the Mona Lisa's eyes seemed to move. The face was neutral in all respects; the expression neither happy or sad, not really female nor male. The image was clearly of a woman, but the face taken alone could have been either gender. The Mona Lisa's face of equanimity looked like many depictions of Buddha.

What's your story? Your secret? Maddy wondered. She imagined the women of that time: laborers or aristocrats, dependent on husbands, restricted freedom of expression and choice, unable to support themselves. The world had changed so dramatically since the sixteenth century, and yet some residual elements remained. Maddy suddenly felt exhausted, overwhelmed with culture and history. She nudged free of the crowd and glanced back to make sure that Richard, still bleary eyed, was in tow.

Three

The train pulled into Sudbahnhof at midnight in the warm Vienna night. They had taken a night train in an effort to save money on lodging, but they had miscalculated and ended up in Austria at midnight. The cavernous train station was empty. White granite pillars held up a massive domed ceiling of glass and iron. The station felt old and substantial, as if it could withstand a bomb attack or weather a great storm. Maddy ducked as pigeons flew in the open arched entryways; the expansive station had no doors. The service counter had closed hours before, like metal teeth shuttered behind wrought-iron grids. The only living presence was the swooping birds. The restrooms were locked tight.

"Our connecting train doesn't leave until six AM," Maddy said. "I could really use some food."

"I could use a drink, and a bathroom." Richard strode beyond the granite-block arch and peered out into the darkness. It looked industrial beyond the train tracks, but one tiny light shown through a small window blocks away.

"Maybe it's a store or pub--should we try it?" Maddy asked.

"Might as well. I can't take a piss here." Richard said.

The 'open' sign was grungy with secondhand smoke. They pushed the door into the thick, smoky pub. Richard dropped his pack and straddled the bar stool looking right at home. Maddy sat one seat down and leaned bare arms onto the smooth worn wood.

"Hello. What can I get you?" The bartender's face was loose and wrinkled and grey hair nipped at his temples. Thankfully, his English was good. They were in Austria on the recommendation of a neighbor couple, Greggor and Anna. Greggor's brother, Helmar, lived in a small village several hours outside of Vienna. Greggor had arranged for Helmar to meet Maddy and Richard and show them the Austrian countryside.

"I'll have a bottle of Cabernet Sauvignon," Richard ordered.

"And for you, miss?" The bartender inquired.

"I'll have a gin and tonic." Why not? She didn't have to drive, only stumble back across the tracks by dawn. Maddy munched on some pretzels and perused her copy of Europe on a Shoe String. Richard made a dent in the bottle of cabernet. Maddy nodded yes to a second drink and felt her eyelids get heavy. It was already one AM and it made no sense to get a hotel, but Maddy longed for a soft bed. She took a long draw on the clear tart liquid and looked over at Richard who was emptying the last of the wine from his goblet. He smiled and threw a heavy arm over her shoulder.

"You gonna stay up all night Miss Maddy?" He slurred,

leaning too close.

She winced under his pressure and breath. "Maybe I'll nap back at the station," she said.

She extricated herself from his clumsy embrace and went to the bathroom. She felt a little wobbly from the two gin and tonics but it was not enough to cover the revulsion she felt by Richard's drunken touch. Sober, he rarely touched her and she had grown accustomed to the space, even comfortable in her bubble, so his intrusion made her feel violated.

It had been different once, early in their marriage, before the baby. After college, Richard had taken a job with a large insurance company and Maddy worked in the HR department of a local hospital. They bought a house and tried to start a family. At least Maddy did. For the first years of their marriage, Richard said that he wanted a child, but when the time came, he changed his mind. They fought about it for months.

Fearing that Maddy would get pregnant 'on accident,' Richard refused to have sex. He had a mountain of excuses that eventually turned into working late every evening. But one night after a Christmas party, when Richard was completely bombed, they slept together. In the morning he did not even remember the encounter, but Maddy did, and knew she was pregnant.

She hid it from him for a few months for fear that he would insist she have an abortion. Finally in early spring she told him. To her surprise he was not mad. He had beamed with pride at his virility. He did a complete about face and seemed genuinely happy about the pregnancy. Richard bragged to his coworkers, called family and shared the happy news while Maddy vomited and nibbled on crackers.

She was pleased that he acted excited, but was soon disappointed when he refused to go to doctor's appointments or prepare the spare room for the baby's arrival. He made it clear through his actions that despite his pride, this was her child, her burden. So Maddy decorated the baby's room. She read books and bought clothes. She lived her own bubble of joy at the impending arrival.

At seven months Maddy was bursting with baby and beginning to move slowly in the summer heat. She waddled around the grocery store and got knowing nods from the experienced mothers in her office. The baby was heavy as she made her way into the doctor's office for her monthly checkup. After the nurse took her vital signs the doctor came in and pressed his stethoscope against her belly and frowned. He moved it around and pressed harder.

"What's wrong?" Maddy asked.

"It's hard to hear the baby's heartbeat," he said. "I'm going to do an ultrasound. As he readied the machine he asked, "Would you like to call your husband or someone, just in case I need to send you for some tests?" His voice was calm but hesitant.

"I'm sure everything is fine." Maddy said with great naivety. But the news went from vague to grave. The ultrasound showed no movement and no heartbeat. The doctor was replaced by a nurse who gave Maddy some papers with an appointment scheduled the next day for the baby to be delivered, dead.

Maddy barely made it home. The shock paralyzed her. She sat with her hands glued to the steering wheel until angry drivers behind her missed the light. At home, she clutched her belly and wept. The deluge of tears would not stop. She tried to get ahold of her mother, but Caroline was out of town and not due back for a week. Calls to Richard's office were forwarded to voicemail. Maddy sat alone on the couch all day and into the night, holding her belly, praying and bargaining and willing her child back to life. Richard came home after dark smelling of beer. He had not checked his voicemail and had gone out with some friends for nine holes of golf after work.

When Maddy told him that the baby had died, he flew into a rage. He accused her of doing something to jeopardize the pregnancy and told her he was right all along—that it was never a good idea. Maddy cried until there were no tears left. In the morning Richard drove her to the hospital without a word. The baby was delivered. A nurse asked if Maddy wanted to see the tiny infant. "No!" Richard hollered. "She doesn't need to hold a dead baby." Maddy was so grief stricken she could not muster the energy to challenge him, and so her tiny child, her only child, was taken away unseen.

Maddy went home and ceased to function under the

weight of grief. It was as if a cement truck had poured her body full of concrete. Caroline returned to town and stayed near, to nurse Maddy back to life. Maddy overheard Richard tell Caroline that the baby was deformed and would have been handicapped had it lived. Caroline and Maddy clung tight to one another and grieved until Maddy recovered enough to go back to work. Richard stayed away. He did not speak a single word about the baby or the loss. Maddy never questioned Richard, but she always wondered if the baby was actually normal. She felt in her heart that the tiny girl was whole, perfect.

Maddy washed her hands and face and looked in the pub mirror. Her eyes showed fatigue and alcohol sleepiness but they also held strength. She had made it through the loss of a child and held it together through that horrible time in her marriage. She felt a flicker of self-determination, but the flame was brief and sputtered out as quickly as it had come. She returned to the bar to find Richard staring at an empty glass. Fearful he would order another bottle, she suggested they head back to the station. He was, miraculously, still able to walk even under the weight of his pack, and they made their way through the dark back to the granite cavern of the train station.

Some men had gathered at one end of the station, but having no luggage, they didn't look like passengers. Their voices sounded far away and yet too loud. Maddy flopped down on the floor using her backpack as a pillow. She slept a little, in and out, waking intermittently to the glare of huge sulfur lights and strange voices. Near dawn but still dark, she woke with a headache and sat up to get her bearings. A few people with trunks had come in and sat reading the newspaper, and the men from earlier were now close, too close. Maddy could see that they had formed a perimeter around her and Richard.

"What's going on?" Maddy asked, confused and suddenly alarmed. Her tank top slouched off one shoulder.

Richard turned to look at her. His eyes were bloodshot and exhausted. He looked old and more tired than she had ever seen, but there was a fierceness coming off him as he stood above her.

"These men seemed a bit too interested in you," he whispered to her. "I wish I knew what they were saying-- I don't like how they look."

"What time is it?" She asked.

"Close to five-thirty," he said.

"Did you get any sleep?" Maddy asked.

"No, I've been busy standing right here." He crossed his arms over his chest.

"All night?" She questioned.

"All night," he said.

The ticket window slid back and bathroom locks clicked open as the station came to life. The questionable men melted away into the early morning passengers who began to fill the benches waiting for trains. Maddy watched from her backpack perch as Richard shuffled to the bathroom.

Her husband, from whom she had withdrawn just hours before, had protected her and watched over her so she could sleep. She rubbed her eyes and dug in her pack for a hairbrush. Richard returned and sat heavily next to her.

"Thank you," she said and gently touched his arm. He nodded and waited for the early train to arrive.

Maddy pressed her face against the glass of the sunroom. Rain streamed down the window. She was hung over from the gin and tonic the night before, she was exhausted from the groggy fitful sleep, and she was worn out by Richard's anger. He was exhausted she knew, from standing guard all night, but he blamed her now for arriving in Pottenstein in a full downpour to a locked house and Helmar not at home.

"I called and called but got no answer," Maddy sighed, "What do you want me to do?"

Richard's fatigue made his face crumple, the wrinkles around his eyes collapsing onto his cheeks. Before the trip, she had never felt their age difference, but now the thirteen years seemed to have settled on his face. He stomped mud off his boots. "Damn it. We'll just have to wait."

Maddy leaned against the glass staring at the sleek European designed chairs and the satiny smooth finish on the warm cherry coffee table. She slid along the window to the other side of the sunroom, her feet slurping in the mushy grass-mud. Just on a chance she gave the sliding glass door a shove. It made a slight suction sound then released and slid open. Maddy looked up at Richard in surprise, many panes of glass between them. He grabbed his pack and quickly came around.

"Great job. Let's get out of the rain," he said shucking off his boots and stepping into the warm room.

"Do you think its ok?" she asked.

"I don't really care right now. I just want to be dry and dead asleep." Richard pulled his wet shirt off and leaned out of the doorway to wring it.

"What if we have the wrong house?" Maddy envisioned trying to explain to the Austrian police why she had broken into a strangers home to take a nap. But truly she was too tired to argue or fully contemplate all the risks, so she went in and fell asleep next to the beautiful table.

Hours later she awoke to a face just inches above hers. The face was wide, happy and grinning broadly. Helmar grabbed her in a warm embrace when she sat up. She knew him instantly by his mop of long curls. They had met years ago when Helmar had visited Greggor and Anna in the US, and he greeted Maddy and Richard like long lost friends. Behind him stood his girlfriend, Galiana who smiled sweetly, hands clasped at her chest. Galiana was beautiful in an Ivory soap way with smooth perfect skin and high rosy cheeks. Like Helmar, her face was engulfed in an explosion of loose bouncy auburn curls which fell around her like a spring lilac heavy with blooms.

Galiana and Helmar exchanged words in quick Austrian while Maddy tried to apologize for breaking in.

"It's nothing, it's nothing." Helmar repeated, waving them into the house.

"Come, eat," Galiana welcomed. She invited them into the kitchen.

Maddy sipped strong coffee and watched them cook. Galiana was tall and curvy to Helmar's solid frame, and their crazy curls bounced with every step. They moved in a beautifully choreographed dance from fridge, to stove, to sink, toward one another, brushing near and gliding past. There was a peaceful energy about them and an appreciation of the other; a partnership. Maddy was mesmerized. She had never seen such a beautiful couple, like watching ice dancers. She had certainly never experienced anything of the sort with Richard. Even when they thought they were in love, it was awkward, never fluid.

Coffee mugs were refilled all around and Maddy and Richard accepted savory eggs and toast that tasted of home. They shared travel stories and laughed at language errors and made plans for hiking the next day. By evening Maddy went to bed early, happy, and ready to catch up on lost sleep.

The next morning started with thick coffee and fruit bread. Helmar packed hiking gear and two young girls from next door showed up with jackets and eager faces. Maddy smiled at the beautiful pre-teen girls and was glad to hear they would join the hike. Helmar's sons, Ian and Matteus, who had been with his ex-wife Ezbetta the previous night, arrived ready with boots and excellent manners. Both Galiana and Helmar greeted Ezbetta with a two-cheek kiss. The boys were traditionally handsome sporting wide smiles and Ezbetta's straight sandy hair. Both boys spoke excellent English and quickly jumped into the conversation, relishing the role of translator. Helmar packed his and Galiana's cars with gear and kids. Richard squished into the backseat next to Ian and Maddy rode with Galiana. The whole group headed off to pick up her nephew on the way to the mountain.

The tiny Euro cars caravanned along winding roads as if on a roller coaster. The terrain climbed steeply and fog clustered around trees, wispy and ethereal. They parked in an invisible opening and rolled out. The kids seemed to know exactly where to go and headed into the fog without hesitation. Helmar guided the hike, which did not follow a trail but generally went up. Moisture dripped from dense green leaves that acted as tiny chutes directing the droplets onto their heads. Maddy had frequently hiked in the rain back home and was happy to be back in the forest.

After an hour of walking, Helmar called out for a rest break. Children emerged from the fog and clustered around him like apostles as he magically produced a fantastic spread of food. He pulled out a baguette, longer than the rucksack that carried it, and broke it into crusty, chewy pieces. Helmar sliced thick rings of salami on a dark wood cutting board. Each sandwich was topped with a hearty wedge of stinky cheese. The crunchy, salty, savory tastes were complimented with slices of pears and apples. Everyone stood as if in ceremony, eating and humming the flavors. Next, Helmar opened a huge bottle of water and poured it into each child's cupped hands forming a drinking pond and washing station in one. There was a beautiful effortlessness about his efficiency and the children were engaged, never whining, or seeking attention; just being content and present and joyful.

How different this was from American families, Maddy thought. She recalled countless couples coaxing complaining kids up the trail saying 'we're almost there' every one hundred feet. In contrast, these children were at ease and everyone seemed aware of an inherent sense of roles: Helmar as gentle parent- leader, Galiana as herder, Matteus and Ian as translator between not only languages but between the older and younger generations. The boys moved easily between conversations about travel or politics to playful games with the younger children. It was a family unit in an expanded sense that functioned with organic harmony.

Maddy was moved. She tried to recall if she had ever been part of a family like this. Caroline had been dreadfully young as a parent; three children by the time she was twenty-three. Maddy, the middle-child, knew great love but in a kinetic sometimes frantic framework of a single mother who worked and went to school. Maddy herself was proficient in planning and coordinating, but not with the fluidity and grace observed here. She wondered what type of mother she might have been.

The hike continued up into denser fog until it was impossible to see more than a few feet ahead. At what felt like the crest of a hill, a small wooden structure emerged. A sweet smoky scent lured them toward glowing lights behind high windows.

"Where are we?" Maddy inquired.

"It's a Gasthaus," explained Matteus. "We just hiked up the back side of a ski hill," he smiled. "It's our favorite spot."

The Gausthaus fulfilled Maddy's European fantasies of rich culture and traditional food. The structure was built with thick wood like an oversized cabin. Inside, a blazing fireplace filled the center of the room and blasted out a rush of heat upon entering. Long wooden tables were crowded with mismatched high back wooden chairs, each sporting ornate original designs. Ropes were strung crisscross around the room and jackets, hats, and scarves hung like prayer flags. Helmar stripped off layers down to his t-shirt and tossed his clothes over the line. They all followed suit and found a long table to overrun.

The bartender brought steaming hot pretzels hung on tiny coat racks; coarse salt falling from the golden brown loops. Richard and Helmar drank beer from tall mugs and the kids poured themselves cider. Moisture steamed up from the drying clothes and mixed with the sweet aroma of the pretzels and firewood. Steam fogged up the windows.

Conversation was filled with intensity and connectedness. This was a magical place that welcomed anyone willing to walk to the top. Richard laughed and drank many steins of beer; he seemed happy. Seeing Richard's authentic smile, Maddy was saddened by the volatility of her marriage. If they could only find some level of peace with one another.

They ate until they were full and their coats were warm if not dry. Outside the air was clean and the hike down was easy and loose. The youngest kids fell asleep in the car as Galiana drove the winding road and hummed softly to herself. Maddy rode quietly thinking about the beauty of the children. She could not deny the envy she felt at such a life.

That night the house came to life as people showed up for dinner. Matteus and Ian emerged from the basement freshly showered and helped set up chairs. Helmar's mother, known to all as Oma, arrived with two loaves of hot bread and set about preparing the table. Ezbetta and her fiancé, Wilhelm, hauled in bottles of wine, kissing cheeks all around in greeting. Richard accepted a goblet of wine, but Maddy sat back for a bit to watch this dynamic family.

Helmar and Ezbetta had been married for ten years before divorcing. Each had found another within a year and the family, instead of dividing, multiplied. Matteus and Ian were the center of this comfortable quartet, who by the look of their interactions, seemed like long-time friends. Conversation bounced around and laughter rose like helium.

Maddy looked at Richard. They were welcomed guests, but in reality they were outsiders. They had never experienced this level of intimacy or friendship as a couple. Maddy could hardly imagine being close friends with an ex-spouse. Maybe Europeans were just better at moving on or accepting change. Matteus saw Maddy sitting apart and came over next to her. He seemed so composed for a sixteen year old.

"Have they always been such good friends?" Maddy nodded toward his parents and their partners.

"It was hard for a bit when they first split, but they realized they could still love each other in a different way and be friends." Matteus smiled as he caught a wink from his father who raised his glass in a gentle salute.

"It's quite remarkable," Maddy mused. "Most families come apart over a divorce."

Matteus shrugged, "My dad says love changes shape and direction, but it doesn't go away."

Maddy was humbled at the immense wisdom of this young man. They pulled their chairs up to the table to join the conversation.

The next morning Helmar buzzed down the narrow road on the way to drop Maddy and Richard at the train station.

"Where will you go from here?" Galiana asked, as Helmar made a hard turn into the parking area.

"Greece and Turkey." Richard replied.

"Oh--I love Turkey," Galiana invoked. "Did you know it

is where Rumi spent most of his life?" Her eyes were filled with a dreamy essence as she spoke.

"Rumi," Maddy asked, "Who's that?"

"He was a prolific spiritual poet from the thirteenth century." Galiana said with tangible enthusiasm.

"You should try to find his poetry when you are in Turkey, it is beautiful." Helmar added.

Maddy pulled out her blue leather journal and jotted down 'Rumi" for future reference. They all climbed out of the car and hugged goodbye. Maddy thanked them for the hospitality. Helmar and Galiana stood close together, arms wrapped around each other and waved as Richard and Maddy slid away on the train.

Four

The large passenger ferry rocked as it came into port. Maddy riffled through her travelers checks astonished at the dwindling stack. The tariff to enter Turkey from Greece was steep since the two countries had a long history of disagreement and taxed entry and exit at retaliatory rates.

She had slept for an hour on the rocking vessel and woke groggily to passengers milling about and filling out entrance papers to Turkey. A young woman plopped down next to Maddy and frowned over the embarkation form.

"Excuse me," she said. "What do I put on line seven if I don't know where I am traveling to, or where I am staying?"

"Just pick a city," Richard answered, "and pick a hotel from the guidebook--nobody cares. It's just bureaucratic paperwork."

"Where are you going?" The woman asked. Wavy brown hair framed her bright grey-green eyes.

"I don't really know yet," Maddy paused. "Some backpacker hotel in Izmir for a few days before heading to Istanbul."

"Can I share a ride with you?"

"Sure." Maddy smiled, happy to have some company other than Richard.

"I'm Chrissy," she grinned and offered her hand.

Many people traveled solo in Europe but Maddy had been surprised at the number of women she had met who were traveling alone. It was clearly a great way to meet other travelers and see the world but it also seemed risky and unknown.

"Where are you from?" Maddy inquired of Chrissy.

"Seattle, Washington."

"No way--we're from Bend, Oregon."

Chrissy squealed and hugged Maddy as if they were long lost friends. It was like being in kindergarten where the smallest commonality actuated best-friend status. Being far from home evoked an instinctual need for connection, especially given the void Maddy always felt with Richard. A girlfriend, if only for a few days, was welcome.

They were corralled into customs lines, ushered off the boat and cued up once more before eventually getting passports stamped. Out in the street the threesome was greeted by a hoard of hotel hawkers. Cabbies and porters fought for fares and hustled groups of travelers into beat up Datsun mini sedans and whisked them off in all directions. Their compact taxi was equipped with neither seatbelts nor turn signals and used centripetal force to keep everyone in place. Maddy was pressed hard to both Richard and Chrissy as they hurtled through the narrow streets of Izmir. They passed construction zones and open markets with meat dangling from hooks. They whizzed by mosques whose prayer calls filled the air. At intervals, aromas of roasted lamb permeated the car while Maddy tried in vain to see where they were going. After several gyrating turns down increasingly narrower streets, the car screeched to a halt and they were abruptly dumped out in a heap of bags and Turkish Lira in front of an ancient stone building, which now housed a youth hostel. Chrissy grabbed Maddy's hand and ducked into the thick rock doorway.

At the front desk, they checked in and were assigned a bunk in separate men's and women's dorms. The lobby teemed with travelers and languages hung in the air like perfume. Maddy scanned the walls plastered with posters advertising day trips, guided cycling events, ancient ruin walks, and museum tours. One board highlighted the hostel events which included music night, a rooftop cook out, and a talent show. Maddy beamed with excitement. This was her first true backpacker hostel. She and Richard had stayed in small motels and guesthouses along the way, but this was a true hostel. Maddy and Chrissy left Richard to fend for himself and headed off to the women's dorm to shower, unpack and explore.

The view from the roof was spectacular, overlooking an expanse of the Mediterranean that swept north along a dazzling coastline and blended into a paradoxically ancient and yet modern city. Mosque domes glinted in the sun. High-rise hotels jutted up as testimony to the recent boom of the emerging tourist business. Izmir's proximity to the

Greek islands made it a perfect stop for travelers traversing Europe. Maddy and Chrissy lounged in the sun surrounded by tall, leafy rooftop plants. Backpackers sat at long tables eating, playing cards, and studying maps. Maddy closed her eyes and listened to the symphony of languages and dialects that filled the patio. She was enjoying the liquid cream of a French conversation when Richard jagged in.

"I've been looking all over for you." His voice was tight with controlled annoyance so as not to appear impolite in front of Chrissy, but Maddy knew his tone.

"We're just enjoying the view and the sun," Maddy replied.

"Let's go down and figure out what we're going to see while we're here for the next few days," Richard suggested.

"Chrissy and I thought it would be fun to see some open markets and we definitely want to go to the talent show tomorrow night," Maddy said.

Richard's eyes flickered with anger at being left out of the planning, but sensing a united front, he pasted on a fake grin.

He looked around the patio and saw no open seats. "Meet me in the lobby in an hour for dinner," he said and strode off.

"Looks like I might need to give you some space tonight," Chrissy said.

"No." Maddy replied. "I'm enjoying your company. He will just have to get over it." Maddy lifted her chin to punctuate her defiance.

"Ok, but let me know when I need to scat."

Chrissy was a happy, confident person; clearly she had to be for what she was doing. Traveling in Turkey was just a vacation on her real journey to the Peace Corp in Africa. She had just finished her masters in anthropology at the University of Washington and felt that the Peace Corp would be a great opportunity before settling down in a job. She had been assigned to build a school in Gabon. She treated Maddy to stories of learning French and studying construction and architecture to help prepare her for the job. It didn't hurt that it was a nice way to defer her student loans for a few years. Maddy was enthralled with Chrissy's courage and self-reliance and wondered if she would ever be able to do something so challenging, so independent.

The sun was leaning on the edge of the patio when they went back to the women's dorm to change for dinner. Maddy, in an attempt to be respectful of the local customs, put on a long, loose dress she dredged up from the bottom of her bag. In the lobby, she heard Richard's boisterous voice before she could see him. He was talking with two Spanish travelers. Their accents were deliciously thick and perfectly accentuated their manes of jet black hair. Richard turned as Maddy approached, Chrissy a few steps behind. Maddy relaxed when she saw Richard's broad smile.

"Hey there," he beamed. "These guys have invited us to join them for dinner tonight." Maddy smiled. Richard was essentially a child; happy when included, mopey when left out.

"Perfect," she replied and leaned in close to Chrissy, who whispered, 'crisis averted' out of the side of her mouth. Maddy had confided to Chrissy about her challenges with Richard.

Dinner was a dazzling array of spices: cumin, cinnamon, pepper and garlic. The whole party crammed into a tiny corner table and ate savory Lahmacun (thin Turkish pizza), Talos Boregi (phyllo dough filled with spicy meat and vegetables), Patlicanli Pilav (rice with eggplant), and lamb kebab, washed down with strong Turkish coffee and mint tea. Afterwards, they lumbered back to the hostel, thick with food and laughter.

That night, the rain moved in like uninvited relatives. Drops started as a soft patter around midnight and gained momentum, pounding hard and fast as the night wore on. By first light, the rain had saturated the rooftop gardens and pooled on the empty patio tables. Sheets of rain were still falling when Maddy and Chrissy met Richard in the lobby. By now, he had accepted their fast-track friendship and greeted them both warmly. Ideas were batted among the trio before deciding to brave the rain and see a world renowned spice market on the north end of the city past the port. Armed with directions and rain coats, they headed out into the narrow streets to reach the main road and catch a cab. The rain pummeled Maddy's coat and dripped down onto her thin cotton pants darkening the light tan cotton to a wet brown above her knees. The stone streets were slippery and Chrissy held onto Maddy with one hand and the sleeve of Richard's jacket with the other as they hopped over huge puddles in the narrow back streets. The water filled every crack and pothole of the bumpy road and gathered along the edges into tiny rivers. The short, channel-like street ended in a T and they turned at the bottom of the hill. The pooling water crested over Maddy's shoes as she stepped off the sidewalk.

"It's a swimming pool down here." Maddy sloshed in the ankle deep water that filled the entire street. She wiped rain out of her eyes and looked around. "Maybe we should go a different way, I don't like this," Maddy said.

They agreed unanimously and took the next left onto another skinny cobbled street. A small plastic toy with tiger stripes floated down the road in the rising water that submerged Maddy's feet completely.

"This is starting to worry me," Chrissy said, alarm rising in her voice. Her legs cut turbulent channels in the rushing water. Chrissy pushed sopping wet curls back from her face and wiped the hard rain from her eyes in time to sidestep a small wooden hand cart that tumbled past in the current. Residents leaned out of windows shouting and pointing in every direction, their Turkish calls muted by the rushing roar of the rising flood.

Richard squinted in the pelting rain and grabbed onto both Maddy and Chrissy and yelled, "We have to get out of here-- it's like a slot canyon." Chaotic voices bounced everywhere.

"Go toward the wall," Richard directed. "We need to get

ahold of something solid."

The water rose with every step and made them move in slow motion. They locked hands and struggled for balance as they forced their way against the swelling water. Richard grunted and pushed them forward. Twenty yards up a man stood in an open doorway; his long, maroon shirt bled color into the rushing waters. He waved at Richard, motioning them toward his home. Maddy saw three other Turkish men arrive and form a human chain; arms linked with the heaviest man as the anchor braced in the doorway. Water crested the men's waists.

Richard turned and put his face close to Maddy's and said, "When we get close enough, I need to grab his hand. You are going to have to let go of my hand and take my coat."

"Noooo!" She screamed, barely keeping her feet beneath her.

Near the doorway, Richard ignored her protest and yelled, "Now!" He shoved Maddy's hand into his coat pocket then wrenched his wet fingers from her grasp. Maddy caught the zippered seam and panic glued her hand to the fabric.

Richard pushed hard for two steps as Maddy fought to stay close and upright, but Chrissy lost her footing altogether and spun like a windsock attached to Richards coat; her feet kicking helplessly against the river. Richard locked eyes with the Turkish rescuer and stretched his arm toward safety. The men in the doorway leaned out with more hope than reach.

"Push! Push!" Richard bellowed. Maddy tried to help, but she slipped and her feet left the ground. Richard, feeling the pull of Maddy on his coat, grunted in a final cathartic effort. With one heaving lunge, he grabbed the man's hand. The anchor man reeled in each of his comrades, then Richard, followed by the swirling Maddy and Chrissy tethered to Richard's jacket. In a pile, they crossed the threshold out of the torrent and bobbed in the flooded entry. Small tables sloshed up against the walls and bounced off a reed basket that had once sat passively on a red and gold woven rug. The rug floated below the surface of the water like a marooned aquatic creature. Richard slumped, struggling for breath, supported by the anchor man. Maddy shivered against Chrissy, who stood in silent shock.

The rescuers pushed the front door shut. Before the door closed, Maddy caught sight of a dark blue Datsun floating down the hill. Their host motioned everyone upstairs where his wife guided Maddy and Chrissy to the kitchen. She wrapped them in dry cloth and sat them next to the stove. Richard stayed with the men, who plied him with hot apple tea and recapped the event in great animation. Turkish was not a language that Richard had heard before, even when living abroad, and the hosts spoke no English whatsoever, leaving pantomime the only real communication. The Turks gestured wildly and Richard could see the story of 'saving the Americans' being told for generations to come.

Exhausted, Maddy and Chrissy sat and watched two young girls play with a set of dolls while their mother made tea and shuttled it to the men. In an hour the rain stopped and the water receded leaving the street heavy with mud and strewn with furniture. Grateful for both the rescue and the hospitality, Maddy, Chrissy, and Richard thanked their hosts and waved goodbye, sloshing away in soggy shoes. Stiff with post adrenalin legs, they walked back to the hostel.

Maddy rested in her bunk and stared at the saggy mattress above. She was numb from the rain and the near drowning. She was thankful to Richard for taking charge and saving her life. She winced at the thought that it was only a few weeks ago that she had fantasized him as a mummy. Their relationship had always been an emotional teeter totter. At times he spoke to her like his mouth was filled with vinegar, then he would turn around and protect her. She couldn't get a bearing on his true feelings for her. Did he act out of a sense of duty or did he actually care for her? A hollow feeling held residence in her heart. She must be a terrible person for imagining him dead.

The next morning they grabbed an early bus and headed north. The driver passed on blind corners and swerved through traffic for hours before Istanbul emerged like a radiant jewel on the Bosphorus Straits. The sun hung high in a shockingly blue sky above the dark sea.

"It feels like the Emerald City." Maddy said as they navigated toward the city center past beautiful mosques and stone carved buildings decorated in gold and silver.

They got off the bus in an old section of town and followed the guidebook directions toward a popular hostel. Chrissy walked and watched. She had been quiet and contemplative since the flood. In the bright sun, she stood still with wide eyes and admired the juxtaposition of ancient and modern architecture. They passed a park filled with benches and pathways and homely gardens outlined by low stone fences. Women in black burkas sat in the sun. Deep ebony eyes animated by dark lashes peeked out from behind the flowing black cloth. Maddy had read that Muslim women often wore expensive jewelry and ornate under garments beneath their burkas and she wondered what it felt like to have that secret beauty enshrouded in black robes. A pair of young women with exposed faces wore white head scarves wrapped tightly around their smooth cheeks. They giggled, faces close together and Maddy watched as they simultaneously maneuvered wads of sugary bubble gum into place and blew luminous pink bubbles the size of grapefruit. Chrissy beamed as the bubble blowing contest ended with soft pink pops and the two women tumbled into fits of laughter.

Maddy, Richard, and Chrissy checked into a guesthouse located next door to a bakery. The smell of warm bread filled the air. In the lobby, travelers lifted their noses to take in the universal smell of home. After settling their gear, they headed out into Istanbul proper with guidebooks in hand. This vibrant two-continent city stretched out along the Sea of Marmara and buzzed with a collision of color, culture, and architecture that blended the historic Middle Eastern culture with a European feel. In the open squares, street vendors dressed in regal jackets and bright red pantaloons poured hot tea from enormous pots worn like backpacks; they tipped silver swan spouts with theatrical motion to fill each cup to please a gawking crowd. Richard approached the vendor and traded a coin for a cup of steaming mint tea.

They walked along the waterfront past cruise ships and passenger ferries. Busses, brightly decorated in Turkish advertising, weaved in and out of traffic. The spectacular minarets of the Ayasofya Museum came into view.

Maddy stopped and read from the guidebook. The huge dome was made of special hollow bricks. The structure had a main, central dome surrounded by several smaller ones, and four spired towers that rose above a lush green park. Ayasofya had been a Greek Orthodox Church for a thousand years before becoming a Mosque when the Ottoman Turks conquered Constantinople. Maddy stared at the golden dome and felt the irony of hollow bricks beneath a shiny polished exterior.

"Hey, are you ok?" Chrissy called. Maddy realized she was standing in the middle of the street. She ran to catch up.

The museum doors closed behind them sealing out the afternoon heat. Maddy stood for several moments waiting for her eyes to adjust. Blue and red carpets of tribal designs spread out for hundreds of feet in all directions; each rug laid out edge-to-edge. Some were small like prayer mats; others occupied massive real estate on the floor. The mosaic filled the entire domed room.

"Madam, Madam," said a man to the left of the door. "You must cover." He handed Maddy a length of cloth and pantomimed wrapping it around her waist. She thought it was odd that she needed to cover up in a museum but she did as requested. It did feel like a mosque. Alcoves adjacent to the center room revealed the history of the iconic building, how it had been won and lost to one religion after the next. The stained glass windows felt like those of a Christian church but Maddy wondered if stained glass was also used in Islamic design.

They spent the afternoon in the museum learning about the Ottoman Empire, Turkish history, and the array of ancient religions that combined to form modern Turkey. Istanbul was a melting pot of secular and religious life. Some women dressed in western-style clothes while other opted for headscarves and burkas. Modern modes of transportation drove past stone buildings of primeval design. Maddy could feel the tug of the past and the future in a single moment.

As the sun went down, they slowly walked back to the guest house past the waning street markets full of last minute fishmongers and boatmen. The day closed with a loaf of fresh bread slathered in butter. Nothing tasted more like home.

Fog nestled between buildings the next morning as Richard got directions to the Grand Bazaar, a mammoth labyrinth of shopping stalls and food vendors on the must-do list of Istanbul. The motor cab dropped them off in a bustling hub of shoppers at one entrance and the driver cautioned them not to get separated in the serpentine streets. The market was a visual feast and olfactory extravaganza. In a spice-sellers stall, bright milled turmeric was heaped next to fire-orange paprika, black pepper, and white crystal sea salt being sold by the scoop. Adjacent stalls sold powdered cloth dyes that looked like a box of Crayola crayons of periwinkle blue, royal red, marigold, and every hue of pink.

Maddy and Chrissy walked as if in a dreamscape taking in the giant bins of figs, green and black olives with their musky scent, dried apricots, currants, and sweet, sticky raisins. Swarthy, dark-eyed men in crisp slacks and silk shirts beckoned to them to come see their wares or have a cup of tea. Maddy caressed the intricate beadwork on the pointy-toed slipper-shoes lined up stall after stall. They looked magical, adorned with a shimmer of emerald and ruby beads painstakingly embroidered into dizzying patterns.

"Do you think I could get these home in one piece?" Maddy asked, holding up a turquoise slipper emblazoned with amethyst beads.

"They are absolutely beautiful," Chrissy sighed.

Maddy tried to see herself at home in their old house

wearing these coveted shoes. The house was empty and she couldn't place herself; the disembodied shoes floated along the floor of the echoing rooms. Maddy shook her head to clear the dissonant image.

Richard was deep in a stall flipping through a stack of rugs. He loved Persian rugs and Maddy knew he would be there for a while. She wandered further and bought a cone of figs. She shared some Turkish delights with Chrissy; the sticky apricot candy glued together their teeth. They wandered past the gold merchants and fabric vendors, checking back with Richard periodically. It was late when he emerged from the rug stall drunk on tribal history and the symbolic stories told in the designs. The trio wound around the labyrinthine bazaar until they found a sunlit opening that ushered them back into the street full of busy traffic.

On the morning of the last day in Istanbul, Maddy and Chrissy went for a Turkish bath. They took a tiny cab to an ancient wedge of the city and stood with hesitation at the entrance. Maddy stared at the block-cut archway door within the towering structure that rose in a perfect architectural line to a domed peak. Chrissy pushed on the cool, heavy metal door and it swung inward on iron hinges. They stepped into an open entry furnished with simple chairs. Faint, hushed whispers echoed as if from deep within the walls. Maddy looked at Chrissy and saw an excited gleam in her eyes.

"Are you sure about this?" Maddy asked.

"Absolutely," Chrissy replied.

Just then, the pale yellow curtain at the far end of the room opened and a sturdy older woman emerged.

"Pay here. Sit." She said matter-of-factly and pointed to the small wooden chairs. They laid Turkish Lira on the counter and sat obediently. The woman disappeared and then returned with a stack of towels, long thick bathrobes, and a pair of rubber flip flops for each of them.

"Go through there--undress. Put on robe and wait." Her English was clipped but clear and she exited abruptly before questions could be asked.

"Wait for what?" Maddy whispered. Chrissy shrugged, giggled and breezed through the yellow fabric. They undressed and pulled on the Amazonian bathrobes. Maddy gathered folds and folds of fabric around her like a Shar Pei and sat next to Chrissy on the hard wooden bench.

"You fly out to Italy tonight?" Maddy asked quietly trying to hold back the sadness in her voice.

"Yes, I have a week in Rome before heading to Africa."

Maddy looked at Chrissy's thin fingers. Chrissy was so young and petite, but had a palpable confidence. Maddy gazed at the floor, hoping to absorb whatever she could from Chrissy before it was too late.

"Does it ever scare you to travel alone?" Maddy asked.

"Once in a while it's hard," Chrissy said. "But everywhere I have been I've met great people. That makes it easier." Chrissy reached out and took Maddy's hand.

"Don't forget your amazing adventures," Maddy said.

48

"Like almost drowning."

"Almost," said Chrissy. "My thanks to Richard on that one." She smiled at Maddy.

"Yes, Richard." Maddy starred at the floor.

"Don't be sad." Chrissy said hugging her in close. "You have so much to see on your trip."

"It's been great to travel with you." Maddy blinked.

"As a distraction?" Chrissy asked.

"No, as a friend." Maddy defended, then admitted, "Yes, and a buffer."

The stone floor was cool and the cloistered hallway had the privacy of a convent.

"I wish I were brave like you, to travel on my own without Richard. I often wonder what my life would be like without him," Maddy said.

"Do you love him?" Chrissy asked. The question blunted against the dense stone and hung in the silence.

Maddy shifted to pull her robe around her, avoiding both the question and Chrissy's eyes. The robe slid off one shoulder as she gathered it again. "Who in the world are these robes made for?" Maddy asked.

That question was answered as the thin pale curtain was flung acutely aside by a humongous woman wearing tremendous white cotton underpants, and nothing else. Maddy, stunned and amazed, tried not to laugh. She recalled her mother's reference to this type of underwear from a childhood book. Maddy remembered her mother reading about Mrs. Pig's Panties. The woman had steel wool grey hair pulled back in a low bun and her pendulous breasts swung well below the cotton waistline of her massive undies.

"Come." The hulking woman commanded and submerged back through the curtain.

This time Chrissy gave Maddy a "you go first" nod then, capitulated when Maddy shook her head. Maddy held onto the tail of Chrissy's robe and followed through a dark hallway. The dim corridor dove deep into the building before opening onto a spectacular room. Fully clad in white marble, the chamber centered on a gurgling fountain. Towering marble pedestals, like Roman columns, held up a circular domed ceiling. A mosaic of colored glass filled the peak of the dome and filtered rainbow sunlight onto the fountain. Curved marble benches surrounded the fountain. The brutish woman pointed to a row of hooks and shelves and pantomimed 'undress.'

Maddy and Chrissy had shared bedrooms, bathrooms, and a near drowning experience, but in the openness of the white marble room Maddy felt very exposed. Their guide motioned for them to follow her into a steamy antechamber. Chrissy abandoned her flip flops and padded silently into the mist. As Maddy rounded the fountain, she noticed a woman, laying, wet and nude in the filtered light. Droplets of water hovered on the surface of her creamy brown skin. Her face rested in the repose of equanimity.

Maddy entered the steam room and lay down at the

command of their bare-breasted attendant. Warm jets of steam rose from the bench, the floor, and the base of the walls filling the room with viscous moisture. It coated Maddy's body and hair and ran off in rivulets where it condensed. She could hear Chrissy breathing deep lungful's of wetness; it felt like being returned to an embryonic state.

After an indeterminable amount of time, the attendant parted the steam with her bulk and said: "Come out now." Maddy roused dizzily and could feel the pruney ridges on her finger pads as she gripped the slippery marble bench to sit up. In the main chamber there were now two underwear-clad women, one each for Maddy and Chrissy. Maddy approached with apprehension not knowing what was going to happen or how to interact in this foreign space. She laid down and tightly closed her eyes.

The woman donned a scrubbing glove the size of a catcher's mitt and scooped up a handful of a speckled abrasive from a metal bowl. She started on Maddy's legs and rubbed with enough friction to light kindling. She scrubbed in fierce strokes on her thighs, arms and belly, hands and feet. Maddy half expected to see blood when she turned onto her stomach but instead, her skin was intact and shiny clean. The woman exfoliated Maddy's legs, buttocks and back with great force leaving her muscles slightly sore and her skin tingling. She nudged Maddy toward the shower spigots to rinse off. Chrissy was already there and looked pink and slick as water slid unimpeded down into the marble drain.

Upon returning to the slab, Maddy found her scrubber seated on a small wooden stool with a container of oil. In a blur of hairy forearms, the woman massaged warm oil into Maddy's newly exposed skin. It was like being beaten with warm, oily pillows; slightly uncomfortable, mildly comical, but generally relaxing. The oil rub was followed by soap in a frothy lather from head to foot. She kept her eyes tightly shut for fear of them being rubbed with soap and so as not to see just how close her face was to the woman's dangling breasts. Maddy was sent for another shower while Chrissy was seated on the edge of the fountain having her hair washed. She smiled at her friend as golden shampoo was rubbed into a giant froth atop her head like a cartoon character. The grime of backpacker travel washed away in the swirl of suds. The washer grabbed a hefty silver bowl to scoop water from a flowing aqueduct inside the fountain. She poured pan after pan over Maddy's head in a relentless waterfall. Maddy sputtered under the initial drench then quickly got into a rhythm of breathing between bowlfuls.

The final coat was a thick creamy lotion applied like butter in long swaths over every inch of skin. Relaxed and slippery, Maddy was fearful she would slide off the stone bench. She reached out to grab the edge but her hand did not contact stone. Instead it collided with the bather's huge breast that hung down next to the marble slab. The droopy pontoons were closer than she had feared and now she had accidently touched the stranger's boobs. Maddy tried to quiet the 'oh crap--oh crap' in her brain by nonchalantly pulling her hand back up, only to graze the tip of a rough ridged nipple on the way. Maddy's eyes flew open. She searched the woman's face for emotion and tried to express her apology but the bather just continued to slather on the lotion. Without pause or comment, the woman spread the lotion up Maddy's belly and over her breasts. Maddy felt her whole body blush. Well, now we're even.

With heads wrapped in bulky towels, Maddy and Chrissy were left to lie in the filtered light next to the fountain.

"Hey Chrissy," Maddy whispered, "Did she lotion your boobs?"

Chrissy snorted, "Totally, and hers kept thumping against my thigh the whole time."

They both laughed and a flood of relief washed over Maddy, but her laughter turned to a sigh just before she uttered, "The sad part is, that's the most I've been touched in a long time."

The domed room was silent and Maddy lay still; the heat of her admission flushing her neck. When they rose to get dressed, Chrissy embraced Maddy in a tight hug, their clean bodies pressing together. "Everything will be alright," she said.

Maddy nodded. Her skin tingled from the contact with Chrissy's clean body.

Five

The flight on Air Egypt, whispered to be nicknamed 'Scare Egypt' lived up to its name and Maddy's attempts at composure quickly gave way to panic. The take-off pitched her hard against the seat back and Maddy let out a shriek as the plane seemed to climb straight up.

"My God, there are no mountains here, what are they doing?" She panted.

Richard shifted so his back was toward her. The flight attendants stayed buckled tight and did not come around to offer sweets or comfort. Maddy pressed her hands over the top of her ear plugs and tried to shut out the world. The aircraft finally leveled out but Maddy was already spent. She cried for having left Chrissy at the airport, she cried for fear of death over the Mediterranean, and she cried for having to face traveling alone with Richard again.

When the plane landed just outside Cairo, the crew rolled a long staircase up to the door and opened the hatch. Heat like the fires of hell consumed the plane. It sucked the cool, conditioned air straight out of the cabin and everyone's lungs all at once. The hot air was filled with pollution and dust and instantly stole away the moisture that had been rubbed into Maddy's body earlier that morning. Outside, she squinted in the harsh light and scanned the landscape for relief. It was nothing but desert. The sun was obscured by pollution and the harsh air burned her throat. Maddy went limp. Richard shook his head at her. He guided her through customs and into a cab toward the heart of Cairo.

The heat and dust were suffocating and even Richard fanned himself vigorously. The cab driver took them to his sister's-friend's-uncle's-cousin's guesthouse on a busy street where Richard dragged Maddy into the sweltering lobby of a shabby hotel. Men in long sleeved shirts, apparently immune to the heat, moved through the lobby speaking a sharp sounding Egyptian dialect. Things did not improve when Richard opened the door to their cramped room. A wimpy ceiling fan lilted impotent wisps of hot air about the room and greying sheets covered a paper thin mattress. Maddy wailed like Lucille Ball. Richard, now out of patience, threw his arms into the air and left. He returned an hour later with a plan.

"Would a little air conditioning help?" he asked. His mouth held in a firm line.

Maddy nodded. "It's just that I was so clean and cool this morning--I wasn't ready for all this." She looked around the disconsolate room equipped with one high window filtering dirty light from the afternoon sun.

"And Chrissy is gone," Richard said looking directly at

her.

Maddy nodded. She had enjoyed the respite from fighting with him. She reminded herself that everything would be fine once they got to Nepal. She wanted to believe that trekking in the beautiful, spiritual mountains of the Himalayas would restore her heart and renew their relationship. But this was not Nepal. The heat felt like she was hell. Just then, afternoon prayer call began. A loudspeaker outside the window blared to life calling the Islamic faithful toward Mecca. Completely drowned out, they slumped on the bed and listened to the minor key prayer. It was followed by excruciatingly loud music.

Richard shouted at Maddy over the din, "Don't start crying again- we're moving. I found a place with air conditioning and hopefully it's farther from a speaker." He took her hand, turned it over and pressed an international calling card into her palm. "Go call your mom, you're homesick."

The call home was spotty but Caroline was thrilled to hear from Maddy and reassured her that things would get better and cooler as they made their way toward Nepal. Maybe Richard was right about being homesick. The air conditioner in the new hotel churned hard all night and helped block out the 4:00AM prayer call the next morning. Up at six and bleary-eyed, Maddy made her way into the blue-tile bathroom. The floor was actually cool and she thought about lying down next to the sink for a while. Richard was fully awake and thumbing through an Arabic newspaper. His reading glasses sat lopsided on his face.

"Take a look at that toilet," he called. "It's a hoot."

Maddy didn't know what he was talking about. It was a regular American-style toilet except for the small pipe that ran up from the wall.

"Cool," she said. "It has a built-in bidet."

"Yeah, try it out," he said.

Maddy sat, then leaned forward to reach the knob and nearly fell off the toilet as she wrenched the valve open. A jet of cold water shot up behind her like a geyser and splashed down on her back. She let out a piercing shriek. Richard laughed a belly laugh from the other room and she heard his glasses clatter to the floor.

"You jerk, you could have warned me," Maddy said.

"Oh, you'll be fine," he laughed.

She brushed her teeth and looked in the mirror. Their exchange was so convivial, playful almost, that it took her off guard. He seemed so friendly just then. How come we can only be kind to one another in short bursts? Maddy longed for that feeling, that connection, that sense of having a true mate.

She showered and dug through her backpack for something cool to wear. Richard saw her scowling at two dresses, a pair of hiking pants, and some shorts.

Maddy shook her head. "This dress is too short and that one is too low cut. I will die of heat in these hiking pants and I'm sure shorts are taboo." She settled on the longer dress with a low scooping neck and hoped for the best.

Outside, the sidewalks were jammed with people. Men and women were dressed in long sleeves and full length robes. As they passed, men stared openly at her chest. Maddy gathered in the wide neckline of her dress with one hand and held it up around her chin. As they walked to the Cairo Museum, she was bumped and groped at every turn.

"Seriously?" She said to one man that walked straight into her then pressed his body up close while pretending to pass. Richard just shook his head and plowed on through the sidewalk crowd. Maddy considered buying new clothes but didn't have the energy to haggle with a market vendor.

The Cairo Museum was packed with tourists trying to cool off. It was a mammoth structure filled with ancient artifacts of Egyptian history and culture. Maddy recalled her strange fantasy while at the Louvre and decided to avoid the mummy exhibit. How would she explain to Richard any errant grins? She marveled at the display depicting the engineering miracle of the pyramids. She tried to commit the information to mind knowing she would be seeing the pyramids the following day. They lingered for hours in the cool museum to let the afternoon sun pass, and then returned to the dense madness of the city to book a flight to Nepal.

"Every flight is full for two weeks," explained the small travel agent who sweated behind the cramped desk. He had made multiple calls and queried flights on his blue DOS computer screen. Nothing was available.

"I can get you a flight to New Delhi if you have a Visa," he said.

Richard looked at Maddy with a scowl. This had been a big dilemma back home and the source of several fights. Getting an Indian Visa was painstakingly slow and cumbersome. Unable to predict what dates it would be needed, Maddy feared that after going through the complicated application process, the Visa would expire before they could use it. Richard had wanted the Visa, precisely for this reason, but could not convince Maddy that it was worth the cost and energy to apply ahead of time. Now, he looked at her with hard eyes.

"Can we just layover in the Delhi airport and then catch a flight to Kathmandu?" Maddy asked.

"Sometimes yes, sometimes no," the agent breathed heavily. "It depends on the layover time and how gracious the officials feel--they can be very strict, I'm told."

"What other options do we have?" Richard was getting frustrated.

"You could travel south to the Sinai then cross into Israel. I'm sure you can get a flight out of Tel Aviv."

"Can you book that for us?" Maddy asked hopefully.

The agent clicked his tongue and shook his head. "No, I cannot make you a ticket from here, but I can get you a bus to a beautiful resort in Hurgatta on your way. You can enjoy snorkeling and clean sand…" He slid smoothly into his sales pitch and pointed to a poster as if he were Vanna White turning vowels. The poster showed an expanse of crystal sand and deep blue water with a couple holding hands.

"The Red Sea does have spectacular diving." Richard's firm voice had softened and his eyes glittered with excitement.

Maddy knew he loved the Red Sea. He had lived in Djibouti for two years before graduate school. At the time, he had been engaged to a young woman. Jill, thin and beautiful, was wily in a way that excited him. They'd had a whirlwind romance while he prepared to move overseas for a two year work contract. The plan was for him to get settled first in Djibouti. They would meet in Hawaii for a wedding and honeymoon, then apply for her visa so she could join him in Africa. The wedding was quick, just the two of them and some locals to witness. Richard was overtaken by Jill's beauty as she dove topless into the blue waves and sunbathed nude on the black sand beach. They parted at the Hawaiian airport filled with longing to be together soon.

Jill had returned home to await visa approval, which dragged on for several months before it was denied. Richard worked feverishly to reapply on her behalf, insisting that his wife be with him. His solace from the heat and loneliness was diving in the Red Sea. After nine months of rejected applications, Jill took it as a sign. She moved in with another man leaving Richard distraught and melting on the other side of the globe. He survived the rejection by scuba diving. Each night after work he would dive down to cool water and sit until the tank ran low. The experience had left him wary of marriage but in love with the Red Sea.

The sales pitch was complete and both Richard and the travel agent looked at Maddy waiting for her reply.

"Looks like we are headed to the Sinai Peninsula," Maddy said.

They left with tickets for a night bus the following evening and Richard smiled all the way down the block.

The next morning they headed off early to see the pyramids of Giza. The cab driver stopped at three papyrus shops and two tea stands before delivering Maddy and Richard to a herd of mules by the side of the road.

"Too much far to walk," the mule driver said. "You must take mule."

Maddy could see the pyramids in the distance and agreed that a trek by foot over hot sand was undesirable at best. The rocking ride on the mule's back was hot, smelly and slow. In front of the monolithic Sphinx, the mule guide helped Maddy down and brazenly groped her breast as she slid off the animal. The guide was not even subtle and gave her an entitled shrug when she said, "Don't touch me."

"What do you expect?" Richard said. "The US exports Bay Watch all over the world. Other people think western women are immoral and stupid."

"Get me the hell out of this place." Maddy said.

The night bus brought no relief. Middle Eastern pop music blared over grating speakers while the air conditioner dripped on Maddy in the farthest-back seat of the bus. She put a towel over her head and installed pink foam earplugs to try for sleep. Things got worse when the man next to Maddy vomited bootleg mango liquor into the aisle. Richard, who had reached his limit, went up front and had a heated argument with the driver's assistant. Twenty minutes later the bus jerked to a stop and the assistant scooped up a bucket of sand and spread it on the back floor of the bus and called it good.

The vomiting continued when they switched from the bus to a boat in the port of Hurgatta. The 'Hurgatta Resort' looked nothing like the poster and Richard agreed that they should skip it and head out over the Sinai. The boat full of international tourists heaved and bobbed in the turbulent crossing. Rough water just beyond the Gulf of Suez sent passengers to the railings. Maddy employed every remedy in her motion sickness kit: double dose of Dramamine, acupressure wrist bands, earplugs (to drown out the heaving sounds), and ginger candy chews. Even Richard, who loved the water, looked slightly green but remained one of the few people who did not throw up.

Dahab, Egypt, on the Sinai Peninsula, turned out to be a sandy hippie retreat. Open air restaurants lined the beachfront with canvas canopies flapping in the breeze. Groups of Israeli teenagers, on break from their required military service, occupied the ample cushions in the sand-level dining lounges. After finding a room in a stark Bedouin guesthouse, Maddy and Richard crashed onto the oversized pillows, glad to be away from the masses and oppressive heat of Cairo.

They ordered lunch, then tea, then an afternoon snack while they read and wrote postcards to friends back home. By evening, the restaurants were filled and a British couple joined them on the pillow-couches for dinner. Peter and Sarah were from London on a two-week holiday. Sarah had pixyish features outlined by sun-bleached white hair. A nurse back home, she worked the evening shift and whenever possible took time to bask in the sun, thus sporting a cluster of tiny freckles across her cheeks and nose. Peter, shyer than his companion, talked little about his catering and delivery job, but listened and smiled while Sarah shared their stories of snorkeling that day.

Richard listened intently and asked about the best spots for snorkeling and diving. Maddy could see his excitement building when Peter and Sarah said they had signed up for three more trips.

"Tomorrow we're going to the The Blue Hole. Want to come?" Sarah offered. "It's supposed to have brilliant visibility."

"Yes." Richard belted out immediately. "What time-- Where can I meet you?"

Sarah laughed at his eagerness and they agreed to meet at nine.

The Blue Hole was a popular snorkeling and dive spot. It was a protected marine reserve just minutes by car from town. Sarah and Richard talked about fish on the short boat ride out to the reef. Guides handed out gear and gave a brief reminder not to touch the coral and not to take any souvenirs from the water. Maddy struggled with her mask while Richard expertly slid on his gear and was ready to go in seconds. Still working to get her snorkel untwisted, Maddy dropped into the water and treaded frantically to stay afloat.

"You're a sinker." Richard said as she churned at the clear aquamarine water. Richard called to the boat guide who threw him a snorkel vest. He swam deftly back to Maddy and helped her clip in while she spun spindly arms through the water. Maddy had taken diving lessons at the local community college before the trip but was never comfortable in all the gear. She could not relax nor overcome the fear of breathing under water. At least with snorkeling, she was close to the surface. Richard, clearly embarrassed by her lack of mastery, took every opportunity to roll his eyes at her.

"Don't stand on the coral and you will be fine." He swam off toward the crescent-shaped reef.

Maddy stayed on the surface and followed the curving reef while Richard plunged deep to point out rare fish or shoo out hiding creatures from their camouflage. Giant pink sea anemones waved silky fronds that gathered up tiny debris. Richard was so comfortable in the water, part fish, able to clear his snorkel in a single huff. Why didn't he carry that aquatic grace with him to land? Maddy paddled slowly and tried to remember her initial attraction to him. He had been so worldly, traveled and full of stories. She remembered her college roommate teasing her: "You're falling in love," Christina had said in a sweet sing-song voice. Maddy must have looked all moon-eyed and surely deserved the teasing, but now she could not conjure up that feeling.

That evening, among the restaurant pillows, they were joined by Peter and Sarah again and a new Australian couple, Jack and Celeste. Maddy, starving from her snorkeling effort, ate everything in sight, then ordered more. They were all amazed when Maddy ordered seconds of rice pilaf, stuffed pepper and pine nut couscous. Celeste's laugh resonated in her curvy and robust body; her hair a raucous red mane. Jack called her Red in keeping with not only with the hair but her fire for adventure. Celeste spoke with raspy excitement and was quickly invited on the dive boat trip planned for the next day. Maddy opted out having had enough water, and Jack decided to stay back and have a quiet day for himself.

That night, Maddy's stomach took revenge and relegated her to a thankfully immaculate bathroom. She marveled at the ability of the Bedouin women to clean away every grain of sand from the tile floor. Maddy finally fell asleep at dawn and woke mid-morning in a clammy fever; Richard's bed was empty. She dug in her bag for aspirin but found none and was forced to find her shoes to search for a pharmacy. She didn't make it far and must have looked terrible because Amina, the elder Bedouin guesthouse keeper approached and put a hand to Maddy's forehead clicking her tongue.

She called out in Arabic to another woman, then turned to Maddy. "You rest, I bring tea."

Too weak to argue and freezing despite the blazing sun, Maddy returned to bed. Amina brought a pot of strong, sweet, licorice-tasting tea and insisted Maddy drink several cups before she collapsed back to sleep. She slept until the sun tilted and only woke when Richard returned, red with sun and drunk on tropical fish.

"What's wrong with you?" He asked, tracking sand in on his sandals.

"I thought I had food poisoning, but now it's turned into a fever," Maddy explained. "I was up all night." Her hair stuck out in all directions with feverish sweat.

"You look like crap," he said.

"Thanks." Maddy rolled over and went back to sleep.

After Richard left for dinner, Amina brought more tea, a new kind that tasted like dirt. Maddy slept more and woke late. She stumbled to the bathroom under Amina's watchful eye, the night air providing little relief from the heat.

Back in bed Maddy dreamt about impossible problems assigned to her for which she was direly unqualified to solve. She had been named ambassador to a small African country ravaged by civil war and famine. She was employed to coordinate food supplies for hundreds of thousands of refugees on the brink of starvation. The food had been dropped from helicopters in the hot night and she was tasked with its safety and distribution. In her dream, she ran from package to package and tried to drag the heavy boxes back to her hut before daybreak. Desert animals skittered around her feet as she sprinted through the inky darkness to the parachute-dropped boxes. Frantically, she felt around the edges of each crate and strained to calculate the volume of rice needed by each refugee to survive. Tangled in her sheet, she was panting furiously when she woke to Richard's snore and reek of hookah tobacco that sent her gagging to the bathroom.

Cold water on her face felt like liquid nitrogen and made her hands ache in spikes. She dragged herself back to the room, poured herself into her down sleeping bag and quickly resumed her quagmire dream. At daylight, she awoke still shivering. Richard's bed was empty again. She heard a soft knock on the door. Expecting Amina and momentarily blinded by the bright sunlight through the door, she was surprised to hear Jack's voice.

"Hi--Maddy, are you ok?" He asked quietly.

"How are you here?" She shielded the bright light from her eyes.

"Richard mentioned you were sick last night while we were at dinner and I didn't see you this morning when they all left to go diving. The woman here just assumed we were all together because when I came into the courtyard she pointed me here."

He sounded far away but too loud. Jack approached the bed, close to her musty thick fever.

"You need to see a doctor." he said.

"Too tired," she whispered and dozed lightly. She was barely aware of Jacks hand near her forehead before he disappeared into the glare of sunlight.

She awoke again to Amina and Jack talking softly and moving around the room. Her feet were heavy and wet with cold socks, but she could not sit up to take a look. It occurred to her that she might have wet the bed, which was reinforced by a pungent sour smell in the room. She found neither the physical resources nor sufficient embarrassment to propel her out of bed. Amina propped her head up slightly with pillows and nudged at Maddy's mouth with a spoon. Amina ladled small bites of warm, soupy mush toward Maddy. It was buttery with salt but coated in sugar and reminded her of malt-o-meal.

"I have to go home." Maddy said between mouthfuls.

"Shhhhh," Amina hushed and continued feeding small bites. She wiped Maddy's forehead with a smelly cloth.

Maddy pulled back, "Whew--that smells terrible."

"It's vinegar." Jack said. "Amina swears that it breaks a fever when applied to both head and feet."

"You put vinegar in my socks?"

"Yep, soaked them through." Jack smiled.

"Thank God--I thought I wet the bed all the way down to my feet."

Jack laughed. "We're taking you to the doctor after we get a little food in your system."

"Bath first." Amina said.

"Vinegar bath?" Maddy asked.

"At least you're more cogent now." Jack said. "You were muttering something about rice."

"Food aid, refugees, math--it just wasn't working." Maddy said. The dream made no sense to her now.

Amina untwisted wet sheets and gently washed Maddy's neck and arms. Jack removed the vinegar socks and wiped her feet with a clean cool cloth.

"Time now for Dr. Sammy," Amina said.

Maddy felt like a rag doll as Jack maneuvered her to standing and held her steady while Amina wrapped a sarong around her waist to cover her damp flowered undies.

"Let's go," said Jack, hoisting her up close, his hand around her like he might have walked a drunken buddy from a party. With Amina on her other side, they crossed the courtyard passing children who looked up from their marble game at the floppy woman being half dragged across the sand.

Dr. Sammy was a tidy, white shirted man whose office was in a small concrete room sandwiched between a kebab stand and a hokey tourist shop advertising biscuits and ice cream. Dr. Sammy spoke to Amina while he looked in Maddy's throat and felt her neck and feet. He got up and left for a long time; long enough that Maddy needed to lay down again. She accepted a spot against Jack's shoulder. He was slight but softer than he looked and Maddy was grateful for the kindness of this traveler she barely knew.

"Thank you for helping me." Maddy said weakly, dozing. Jack patted her arm.

Dr. Sammy returned with a small package of white pills and gave instructions to Amina. Maddy could hear muffled voices talking about money.

"No, I'm not her husband," he said, "but I'll take care of it. Let's get her back to bed."

Amina and Jack stumbled Maddy back through thin alleys. Heat radiated off the sand and flushed her face. Her eyelids fell shut from exhaustion.

"I'm thirsty," she muttered. Jack nodded and sweated with the effort of half carrying her.

Maddy woke in bed, vinegar socks reapplied. Jack stepped forward and nudged a white pill into her mouth. He brought a cup of cold, bubbly liquid to her lips. Where he had found cold Sprite was beyond her, but she gulped the soothing bubbles to quiet her thirst.

It was evening when her fever finally broke and she heard Jack, Celeste, and Richard talking about the diving trip. Celeste described the deep shelf beyond the Blue Hole that teemed with giant grouper and multi-colored coral. Maddy listened with closed eyes to Celeste's hoarse voice that sounded like Janis Joplin.

"Well, it's about time." Richard said. "You have been out for hours." Her face was cool now and the bed still wet with sweat and vinegar. She felt better despite the layer of salt on her skin. Maddy tried to sit up only to wobble and thump back down onto the pillow.

"Whoa, not too fast," Jack said. "Have some more soda first--you need to refill the tank." He helped her take small sips from the bottle until she was able to sit up without spinning.

"I could use a shower. I smell sour," Maddy said.

"I'll help you," Celeste offered. "You look as pathetic as Jack's patients back home."

Maddy looked at Jack. "Are you a doctor?"

"No, a vet." He smiled.

"I've been saved by the dog whisperer." Maddy smiled. She felt like a dog, with matted hair and smelly breath.

Richard sat lumpish on the bed. His face was tanned deep from hours on the water. Maddy looked at him. He didn't look back.

"Let's get you to the shower," Celeste said gathering things up like a mother hen. Maddy glared at Richard as she stood on unsteady legs. He continued to avert his eyes.

"Useless ass." Maddy muttered as she crossed the sandy courtyard.

"Richard?" Questioned Celeste. "He's not so bad. Loads of fun on the boat, lots of good stories."

"Oh, I'm sure he is," Maddy said. "Half of them made up, all of them exaggerated. The life of the party. Thank God for Jack."

"Yeah," she said, "Jack's a good mate." Her Australian accent rang out.

Maddy slammed her shampoo bottle into the small sink and looked in the mirror. Dark circles framed her blue eyes and her skin hung sallow on thin cheeks, but her hair was the real sight--a spectacular Medusa-banshee look.

"Oh my," she said.

"Don't look," Celeste said. "Just shower."

Maddy washed off the vinegar, rinsed away her refugee hallucinations and tried to let go of her anger. She shouldn't have been surprised by Richard and his unwillingness to give up his dive trip to help her while she was sick. Her mind flashed back to her pregnancy; she should have seen the red flags that waved 'he won't be there for you.'

Her hair was clean but a marble of anger was lodged in her throat. She swallowed hard and tried not to cry while Celeste worked a brush into the wet mop of snarls. Maddy's head tugged and jerked like a bobble head figurine.

When one side of her hair was flat she turned around and asked, "Did Richard pay Jack back for the doctor's bill and medication?"

Celeste paused, the brush stuck in a snare. "No actually, Jack was uncomfortable to bring it up."

Maddy closed her eyes. Hot embarrassment filled her. "What did Richard say?"

72

"He just said, 'hey thanks' and dropped it there."

Tears welled up and leaked out the creases of Maddy's eyes and down her face.

'Hey doll, it's ok. No worries." Celeste said.

"I'll pay him back after I get dressed, then I'll kill Richard and feed him to the camels."

Celeste snorted a raspy laugh. "That old Bedouin woman would help you. She glares at Richard with hexes in her eyes whenever he shows his face."

Maddy got dressed and walked back to her small room but stopped when she saw Amina carrying baskets through the courtyard. Amina smiled a thin line showing crooked teeth; age lines bracketed her cheeks like ripples on a pond.

"I really appreciate all your help." Maddy said. "I don't know how to thank you."

Amina's smile broadened and she hugged Maddy, the large baskets bounced against her back.

"You stay with me tomorrow. I make you better." Amina held Maddy's chin and stared with wise dark eyes.

"I will," Maddy agreed. "And thank you." She squeezed Amina's broad knuckles.

Maddy withheld her eyes from Richard and fished out a small roll of American dollars from her backpack. Turning to Jack, her face red, she thanked him for his help and fitted the money into his palm. He quietly accepted and nodded his head.

"I'm going to get some tea and rice." Maddy announced. "Celeste, Jack, would you like to come?"

Richard brought up the rear like an uninvited cousin.

The diving group went out early the next morning and Maddy was happy to see Richard's bed empty when she awoke. The sun was already blazing. She padded out into the courtyard, still a little weak but feeling better. Amina looked up and waved her over, soapy water dripped from her hands.

"Noora, Alaya, this is the sick girl." Amina said.

Maddy shrugged and gave a weak smile. "Hi, I'm Maddy."

"You like some tea?" Noora asked. She had an exotic face; eyes lined with charcoal above dark lashes. The black eyeliner fanned out in a curving swoop up toward her temple. Her dress was midnight blue with a small flowered pattern and dark hem. It covered her from ankle to wrist. She wore a red head scarf pulled tight across the forehead allowing her long hair to come forward onto her shoulder.

"I like your hair." Maddy said, admiring the deep orange strands braided into the dark brown locks.

"You like henna?" Amina smiled and looked at the other women. "We will make your hair henna."

"Um, ok." Maddy said. She pulled at a strand of her simple brown hair, turning it over and back. Richard was very particular about her hair. Once in college, in an effort to get rid of a waning permanent, Maddy had cut her hair short, an inch all over. It was liberating and felt exultant to the touch but Richard had come unhinged.

"What the hell were you thinking?" He'd said. His face

contorted as if she were covered with open sores.

"It was time for a change." Maddy had smiled. Small silver hoops dangled softly in her newly exposed ears.

"It looks terrible." He'd said and then left for class.

With drooping shoulders, Maddy had shuffled off to her women's studies class where her new look was fawned over at length.

Maddy turned to Amina and said clearly, "Yes, I like henna." Alayah broke into a big grin.

"Eat first." Amina said and handed Maddy a cup of tea and a small plate of biscuits.

While Maddy ate, the women chatted and gathered bottles, basins and brushes, and stacked them onto the courtyard wall. Dishes were cleared and Maddy was beckoned to sit next to Alayah under a small canopy. Amina mixed a thick brick-colored paste with a wooden spoon while Alayah combed out Maddy's hair. Maddy felt soothed in the comfort of the women and although she did not understand their conversation, she felt their kinship.

As Noora spoke, her intricate facial tattoos came to life. One was a small tree shape below her bottom lip, its evergreen fronds fluttered as her lips moved. Her forehead tattoo was a faded eye with short lashes. The tattoos looked impossibly old against her smooth skin. In contrast, Amina's elder face was lined by a faded lace design along her jawline and a single dot at the tip of her nose depicting the loss of a child. Maddy had read that in some cultures, tattoos were used as part of a curative or mystical ceremony and she wondered if there were any tattoos for courage or clarity.

"Can you do a henna tattoo on me? Maddy asked.

"Oh yes," Amina replied. "We have a very special Barak for you." Amina's eyes hinted of sadness.

She started on Maddy's hair with a plop of thick mud and worked it in layer by layer until Maddy's head was heavy and wobbly on her tired neck. It was like being rocked to sleep. While Amina worked on her hair, Alayah sifted through a bundle of small brushes with angled bristles until she found a fine, single point brush. She dipped the brush into the dark red-orange liquid mixture and began to paint. Intricate patterns of leaves and vines bloomed at the tips of Maddy's fingers and wove up and over her wrist. The vines were alive with shoots and fibers and bursts of flowers in orange lace. Maddy's hands were transformed by Bedouin tribal history. Alayah's face was so close to Maddy's hand she could feel her breath as the art unfolded.

Alayah turned Maddy's hand palm up and looked to Amina who spoke a few clipped words with a nod. Alayah painted three dots in a triangle and blew gently to dry the henna.

"What do the dots mean?" Maddy inquired.

Alayah averted her gaze and Amina explained, "They bring magic to you--to bring more devotion from your husband."

Maddy stared at the dots, small eyes that winked in the

tiny creases of her palm. Did she want his devotion? She loved the exotic feminine of the vines and flowers on the back of her hand, and the inclusive feeling of sharing in these women's traditions, but the symbolic devotion in her palm was empty. Alayah's eyes were dark, brows hunched as she watched Maddy,

"You don't like this?" Alayah said, surfacing Maddy who, suddenly tired, blinked.

"Yes, yes, it's beautiful."

The fatigue of days in bed swept over her and Maddy leaned against the stone wall under the canopy letting the weight of the earthen mud press her down. She was still for a long time, then opened a sleepy eye to see what was tickling her leg. Alayah, with a handful of thread, red, blue, turquoise, and gold, wove a delicate bracelet about Maddy's ankle; nimble fingers darted like a snake's tongue. She added beads to the anklet tassels and tied it off with a minute click as the beads dropped around the bony outcropping. Amina rinsed out the henna from Maddy's hair and toweled it dry under the intense sun. She plaited smooth braids down each side to frame Maddy's face and twisted strands into swirls about her head.

"Beautiful," declared Amina, holding Maddy's face in her hands admiring the transformation. "You go see."

Maddy crossed the hot sand to the bathroom and stood at the mirror. She looked tribal with a bold mane of earthy orange hair. Sleek tight braids blended into the waves. She wiggled her fingers and watched the vines and foliage pulse along tendons like ornate gloves. Thousands of years of Bedouin history suffused her body and she smiled at the face staring back. Awesome. Richard is going to have a fit. She caught a laugh that bubbled up from deep within and burst forth without filter. The strange sound echoed off the concrete walls reverberating in a foreign staccato.

Maddy leaned out the door where all three women waited for her assessment. "Alayah, do you have charcoal?"

The youngest hopped up and grabbed a stub of dark eyeliner. She held Maddy's face to apply a thick line above and below her eyes. Maddy checked the mirror again, pleased by the exotic effect.

"Thank you." Maddy said and turned for them all to see. Amina held Maddy at arms-length, as a mother admiring a daughter before a wedding. She turned Maddy's hands palm up and whispered a prayer before closing her fingers.

Richard stood frozen. The late day sun created a shadow over his face as he stared at someone who looked like Maddy sitting in a circle of women. Amina became aware of his presence and with the click of her tongue, the Bedouin women melted away into the desert scape. Maddy stood. Charcoaled eyes faced Richard directly. She held her back straight and tall, but she leaned a thigh on the wall for support. Its weight reassured her. She could feel her wedding band on her tremulous finger. Her thin blue cotton pants ruffled in the small breeze and she forced herself not to look away, demanding his account. His eyes flitted about taking in her ornamentation.

Richard nodded toward her hands. "Is it permanent?" He asked.

"Semi," she said.

He looked at her fully, head to toe. She wore a loose white shirt that failed to cover her dark nipples. The white cotton created a striking contrast to her black lined eyes and burnt orange braids.

"Well," he said, eyes roving.

She waited. The minutes accumulated between them.

Richard shook his head and turned for the shower, a flowered blue towel flung over his shoulder. She watched his back recede and felt hers slump as adrenalin pooled in her feet and made them impossibly heavy. She had intentionally defied him, jabbed at his aesthetic intolerance. What was she hoping for? An explosive fight? For him to fall hopelessly in love with her? She scrubbed at the three dots on her palm. They blinked back unknowing.

Devotion. Maddy didn't really know what that meant, at least in terms her marriage. She was young when they had met and Maddy recalled being so confident in her decision then. Caroline had begged her to wait, just live together for a while, but Maddy couldn't see what her mother was so concerned about. What would Caroline see now?

Maddy had thought Richard was progressive. He spoke of how he loved her independence, her ability to take care of herself. What she had missed was his idea that if she could take care of herself, then taking care of him would be no problem. She recalled the look of confusion that went over Richard's face during an early marriage conversation when Maddy declared that she was not going to do all the cooking, cleaning, grocery shopping, or child care—she expected a true partnership.

If only a marriage license came with a detailed questionnaire: Who will do what chores? How will money be managed? How often will we have sex? What is your credit score? Your sleep number? She would have been, if not more prepared, at least more realistic. Richard acted as though he was gaining a staff member instead of a wife. Over time, her early independence seemed to slide away as she questioned herself and her marriage. She swiped at the wetness on her lashes and came away with a streak of black.

"What am I doing?" Maddy said aloud to no one.

Six

Getting to Nepal without an Indian visa turned out to be nearly impossible. The only route was to traverse the planet from Tel Aviv to Bucharest to Bahrain to Bangkok to Kathmandu. The plane came into Kathmandu at night, which was a good thing because it spared Maddy the angst of seeing the steep descent over the Himalayas. By the time they got through customs and got their passports stamped, the sun was beginning to rise. Despite her exhaustion and toxic levels of Dramamine, Maddy could not wait to get out and see the city.

Shopkeepers swept away yesterday's dirt with short fanned brooms. Women splashed huge buckets of water onto the street to tamp down the dust and chase away the mangy dogs that sniffed around for scraps. Tibetan prayer flags hung from stubby awnings above metal roll-up garage doors that were leveraged open to display bags of rice and racks of clothes. Some native Nepali faces looked to be either the narrow, more delicate features of Indian descent or the broader stocky faces of Tibetans. The Sherpas seemed a combination of the two. Maddy stopped in the middle of the street and stared at a slight man with ropy legs. He wore cotton shorts, flip flops, and a stained tee-shirt. On his forehead was a wide strap that arched past his ears and descended down around the base of a refrigerator. She watched as he carefully adjusted the cloth padding on his forehead, held the strap in place and slowly, with amazing balance and counterforce, lifted the fridge. Its weight rested on his tilted frame. Methodically, he made his way down the early morning street with careful steps.

Maddy walked down several streets and past a huge covered sign post that functioned as a message board for travelers and climbers. It was plastered with posters selling used ice picks, backpacks, and sleeping bags from climbers who had come down from Everest base camp. Colored paper flyers had backpacker names holding dates and places to meet up, or where to pick up stored gear. One edge of the board was dedicated to lost travelers. Pictures of smiling faces with "MISSING" underneath and approximate dates when the trekker or climber was last seen. Maddy shuddered and remembered her mother's fear that if something happened here, it was possible to go missing forever. It would only take one wrong step to fall off a trail where no one would ever notice. She backed away from the board and went down two doors to a tea shop.

Backpackers emerged from the plethora of guesthouses that filled Kathmandu. Maddy tried to guess the nationality and language of each person who came in for tea. The crowded shop was filled by a large counter and several long tables in the center. She took a seat near the window at the far end of the room. A leggy blond man approached her table blowing on a steamy cup and nodded to ask if the place beside her was taken. When she indicated it was free, he folded himself like a cricket onto the bench beside Maddy. His hair was rumpled, slightly wet, and so blond it was almost white. He had a colossal smile.

"Allo, you must be new to Kathmandu." His accent was thick. Scandinavian? Maddy could not place it.

"How can you tell that I just arrived?" Maddy said before remembering her henna tattoos and burnt orange hair.

He laughed a hearty belly boom. "Your eyes look as plates and you are fresh from somewhere exotic-- Lebanon?"

"Egypt," Maddy said, twirling a strand of her vivid locks. "I almost forgot my new look." She smiled. "How long have you been here?"

"Well," he began slowly, his wide mouth forming rounded words around crisp white teeth. "I came to trek but found myself staying longer--a year now." He held out his hand. "My name is Frederick, by the way, but I am called The Great Dane."

Maddy laughed. How apropos for this towering man. She put her cup down and shook his hand, "I'm Maddy, nice to meet you. What kept you here so long?"

"I met a man with leprosy," he said.

Maddy removed her hand. Frederick raised an eyebrow

in her direction.

"Leprosy, I thought that was eradicated years ago," Maddy said.

"Not so." Frederick said. "It's still a problem here, so I stayed to volunteer at a clinic."

"What do you do there?" She asked.

"I'm a Physiotherapist. I teach people how to adapt to the changes the disease causes."

Maddy scrunched up her brow and asked, "Do people with Leprosy really lose their fingers?"

"Some have deformities from the lesions, but mostly they have weak muscles and numbness." Frederick took another great gulp of tea.

"Aren't you afraid?" Maddy asked.

"Afraid?" He arched the other eyebrow and smiled. "That is what life is about, doing what scares you." His Danish accent made it sound so easy.

"You could come by the clinic and take a look if you like, it's really quite a fun place; the Nepali people are brilliant," he said.

Maddy bent her face close to her tea and took a sip. Did she want to see a leprosy clinic? She set her tea down and looked at the bent page of her Nepal guidebook at the section describing the various trekking routes. Frederick changed the subject.

"Looking for a good trek?" The Great Dane leaned in and stopped the page on Annapurna.

"This is a very popular trek, and for good reason," he said. "The views are unbelievable and the pass truly feels like you have walked into the sky."

Maddy remembered this trek from her stack of reading back home. It was a highly traveled route according to the Lonely Planet guide. The circuit took twenty to thirty days and had a vast network of tea houses to minimize the need to carry food.

"It sounds wonderful," she said imagining the huge mountains and sweeping valley views.

"Go soon before the pass closes. I went up twice last year before I got across," Frederick said.

"Do people get stuck?" Alarm rose in her voice.

"Not if you are sensible and watch the weather." He motioned for her pen and book and flipped through to a circuit map showing the main villages that formed the route through the Annapurna mountain range.

"Here." He circled a dot next to the village of Manang. "There is a trekker's clinic with a doctor who teaches about altitude sickness. Take the class and ask about pass conditions. They will know."

"Did you get altitude sickness?" Maddy asked.

"Not me, but many do--those who try to go too fast," he replied.

"Any other tips?" She probed for more wisdom.

"Are you walking alone?" He glanced at her hand checking for a wedding band. She had taken it off in Egypt. It now sat in the bottom of her toiletry bag.

"No, my husband is with me." She sighed and scrubbed at the devotional dots in her palm.

"Well then, no need for a guide, only necessary if you are walking alone. Just get a permit, a bus ticket, and some rupees in cash; there are no exchange machines in the mountains." He beamed a smile of sunlight.

She fished out her tiny journal and began a short list. He reached for the guidebook and found the city map of Kathmandu. "Here is the volunteer clinic." He circled a corner in the center of the old town. Then he reached for her journal and scribbled out a tiny figure of a man standing atop a mountain. The character held a flag of Denmark. He signed it in a looping scrawl and smiled. Frederick handed the books back and reached across the table to shake her hand.

"Thank you for all the good advice." Maddy stood to give him room. Frederick rose, extracting his legs with long effort. Once standing, Maddy came just above his navel. Frederick looked down, clearly used to this occurrence and waited for her gaze to climb skyward. Eventually her eyes met his gravitational smile and he laughed. His mammoth paw covered her hand in a hearty shake. As Maddy stepped up to the counter to get more tea, she looked back and could still see the brilliance in the giant space he had just vacated.

Maddy walked around for several hours before returning to Tara Guesthouse, where Richard was just waking up.

"Let's get going," he said. "We need to get on line

for a trekking permit." His hair was wet from the shower and matched his damp mood. Despite her secret hopes, it seemed the closer they got to Nepal, the grumpier Richard had become. Maddy hopped in the shower and was ready to go in minutes.

"What are you smiling about?" Richard groused.

"I'm just happy to be here after months of travel," she said. He scowled. Dark eyebrows fell over his brown eyes.

The streets were busy now with bikes and cows and people. Storefronts and street vendors lined the sidewalk selling souvenirs and traditional Nepali clothing. Children smiled and waved at the tourists and accepted coins, but did not outwardly beg. Local women wore thick cotton skirts in layers, red over black over gold. Most wore braids to hold back long black hair. It seemed that despite the number of foreigners in their country, the Nepali people had not burned out on tourism.

Richard stopped to ask a shopkeeper how to find the Consulate office for permits and Maddy stood watching the people in the street. Down the block she saw the Great Dane towering above everyone else. A smile broke across her face and she turned to Richard.

"Why don't you shop for supplies first and I'll meet you for dinner in a few hours. There is something I need to see."

"But we need a permit today," Richard argued.

"We can get one in the morning, let's get supplies today. I'll be back to the hotel by six." Maddy handed him a fifty dollar traveler's check from her bag and sprinted down the street. Breathless, she caught up to Frederick two blocks later.

"Hi," she said flashing a huge grin. She grabbed his arm for support.

Frederick laughed. "You shouldn't run on your first day at fourteen hundred meters. "You will kill yourself."

"Are you going to work?" Maddy asked. "Can I come and see your clinic?"

"Sure, it shouldn't be too busy this time of day. Let's go," he said.

Frederick wove a path into the heart of Kathmandu passing Durbar Square in front of the old royal palace building. The streets were muddy from foot traffic. Dogs and cows mingled everywhere. People bent in reverence and prayer in front of the many temples and shrines scattered about the city. Frederick clasped Maddy's hand with his and led her into a tiny alley and up a short flight of stairs.

"We are here." He pushed open a small wooden door into a simple room that acted as both reception and treatment area for the patients. Frederick waved toward the back of the room at a Nepali woman who looked up from a wooden desk. The room was set up in treatment stations. In the far right corner there were patients lying on cots doing stretching exercise. Frederick walked in that direction. On the opposite side, a nurse wrapped the swollen fingers of a young man; clean white gauze dangled from his hand.

Nearer the door, at a long table, men sat playing a card game, laughing and cheering each time a score was made.

Frederick put down his bag and opened a cupboard filled with a mish-mosh of decrepit looking medical equipment. Wooden crutches and walking sticks filled one side of the closet. Donated wheelchairs with rusted wheels were packed into the other side.

"This equipment looks so old," Maddy said.

"Not so old, just used and worn," Frederick replied. "I have many friends back home that send me wheelchairs as donations. The Nepali patients use them when needed then return them later."

Maddy thought of the rough, pocked, and muddy streets and understood how a wheelchair could quickly come to look so beaten. "What do you do with the patients?"

"I work with them on strengthening exercises, walking with crutches, anything basically to get them more mobile," he said.

"Do they pay you, or is it all volunteer?" Maddy asked.

"They got a grant this year so I get paid a little to cover my basics. I use my savings when I go trekking or travel around Nepal. Everything is so inexpensive that you can live a long time on very little."

"Don't you miss being home?' Maddy said.

"No. I can go home whenever I like, but nothing compares to the joy of helping someone walk again," Frederick said. Maddy paused. She had never done much in the way of volunteer work. She had friends back home that did church work helping the homeless or mission trips to build schools in poor countries. Because she was not part of a church group it had not dawned on her that she could be a volunteer. She admired how Frederick gave his time effortlessly. Clearly it gave him great satisfaction.

"I also get to practice my Nepalese," Frederick beamed. He smiled at a young man who had just come in through the side door. What was left of his foot poked out of an open sandal, all toes were missing. Frederick shook his hand and introduced Maddy to his patient.

Maddy watched as Frederick used Danish-inflected Nepalese to instruct Tshering on how to wrap his foot for padding and then use his heel to balance and bear weight on the disfigured limb. The two men joked and laughed as they worked and Tshering began to take steps with more ease. At the end of the session, Frederick gave him a walking stick to take home for practice. Tshering bowed and touched his forehead to Frederick's hand in thanks.

"Just like that," Maddy said. "No billing, no paperwork?" She recalled the mountains of claims processed by her hospital accounting department each day. It seemed inconceivable that care could be delivered so simply, so purely.

"How long did it take you to master Nepalese?" Maddy asked.

"Just a few months. It's a pretty simple language," he said.

"I took a class back home, but I only recall a few

words." Maddy said.

Frederick smiled. "It would come right back. Besides the Nepali's think it is funny when foreigners speak their language. Mostly we just laugh together."

They made their way out to the street and Maddy thanked him for the clinic tour and introductions.

"Maybe you will come back after your trek. Tshering will be walking like a champ by then." Frederick said. She agreed that it would be nice to see how he was doing.

"All I'm sure of right now is that I need to be walking in the Himalayas." Maddy said.

Frederick bent low and hugged her, then flagged a tuk-tuk and spoke to the driver in Nepalese giving instructions to drop her at the Tara Guesthouse. Maddy waved goodbye and set off for a jolting ride in the equivalent of a Nepalese golf cart.

Two days later, with trekking permits and hiking supplies, Maddy and Richard bumped along a dusty road on the way to Dumre, the Annapurna region trailhead. Maddy considered it a miracle that she and Richard had ended up on the right bus, given that the main bus station was essentially a wide spot in a narrow road just outside of Kathmandu. Hundreds of people milled around in a sea of chaos. Busses arrived and departed seemingly without logic. But some cosmic force was at play, barely trumping entropy that connected travelers with busses to destinations all over Nepal.

After six hours on the first bus, Maddy's bum was numb. The driver finally pulled to the edge of the road next to a metal shed and pounded on the side of bus and yelled, "Dumre!" Bus number two came three hours later. It looked like a gang of youth had stolen it the night before homecoming and tagged it with graffiti. The colorful school bus had been retro-fitted with a roof rack used to carry luggage and the driver's assistant hefted Maddy's pack up top with one hand. She climbed aboard and looked around. Richard was already on the bus. He has stopped speaking to Maddy after she had run off to catch Frederick. Richard had taken a seat midway in the cabin and was flanked by two Nepali teens. There were other backpackers--some with clean looking gear and excited faces, others more grungy and road-wise. Three rows back a kind-faced man nodded to Maddy and scooted over, squishing his friend toward the window. She had never seen so many people stuffed into a bus and could already feel the constriction. She took a sliver of seat and watched more and more people press in. A man sat down to her right on an impossibly small piece of seat and fell asleep. Finally when it was nearly impossible to exhale, the bus lurched forward down a gravel road.

Gravel gave way to dirt which then conceded to mud. The recent rainfall in the low mountain area left the road a soupy mess. The bus lunged and slurped along until the mud sucked the bus to a halt. The driver, his baggage assistants and several Nepali men got out to survey the situation. They discussed the options at length with lots of pointing and nodding. Eventually they set on pushing the bus backward out of the mud hole, then gunning forward again through to the other side. They heaved and struggled to move the weight of the bus until it cleared the mud hole causing bystanders to erupt into cheers. The muddy men climbed on the roof to ride.

In sections of the road the mud was packed into hard ruts and the bus rocked violently side to side in a sickening rolling motion. Maddy, pressed so tight between her seat mates, did not budge, but sat terrified that the bus would flip over into the ravine. Several times the bus rocked to the tipping point where it paused in pre-fall stillness. She couldn't stop herself from making strange guttural noises as the bus rocked up, then her breath stopped completely until the bus teetered back onto the road. The second time the bus stopped Maddy bolted for the exit. She hopped out and splatted down into shin deep sludge. Wanting to get as far away from the bus as possible, she went around the front to look at the road ahead. At the nose of the bus she squelched a shriek and grabbed onto the bumper. Just beyond the outside edge of the tire was a five-hundred foot cliff. Even more terrifying was her realization that the deep ruts in the road were the only things keeping the bus from toppling into oblivion.

Panic filled Maddy's chest and she backed up around the bus to the safety of the gluey mud. She found Richard loitering across the road.

"I'm not getting back in that bus." Maddy said. Her face was drained of color.

"Why?" He asked having forgotten his pledge of silence.

"There's a huge cliff right there." She pointed generally over the edge. "We will die for sure if the bus rocks too far."

"You going to walk from here? You will get to Bhote Odar in--I don't know--two days."

"I don't care," Maddy said. "I'm not getting back in that bus."

Richard shook his head and walked away.

"I'm riding on top." She declared.

"Oh--that will save you for sure," he said.

"Maybe I can jump off before it rolls down the cliff." Maddy envisioned herself making a Jackie Chan leap from the roof just before in careened into the valley. She could see the bus in a slow motion roll off the edge of the road and Richards face pressed against the dirty glass as Maddy jumped to safety. Her vision was interrupted by the driver's call for passengers to re-board.

"I want to ride on top." Maddy told the driver. Richard rolled his eyes and got inside.

"Please madam back in bus," the driver coaxed.

Maddy shook her head. "No, not inside, I want to ride on top."

"No, no, too much danger," he tried again. His face was

dark with sun and deep lines framed his mouth and eyes.

Maddy stood in the wet mud with arms crossed over her chest. The driver spoke Nepali to some of the roof-top men who shook their heads in turn and looked at her. She was sure they were discussing her insanity, but she didn't care. She did not want to die in a jam-packed metal canister. But the driver could tell she was not getting back inside and so finally, two men on the roof extended their arms and air lifted her, like a toddler up onto the roof. The roof rack was shorter than it looked from the ground and backpacks had shifted out to all the edges. Maddy looked around for something to hang onto but there were no handles. She plunked herself down between two packs as the driver gunned the engine out of the mud.

The bus bumped and jolted along the primitive road and leaned deep when it rocked. A huge hole caught one tire and sent Maddy face down on the metal roof. She could see the feet of the men who squatted around her; they seemed at ease and had no problem keeping their balance on the rocking roof. She rode with her nose down, arms and legs fully splayed. But the increased surface area did nothing to provide more traction and Maddy slid around like a starfish without suction cups. Her hands and feet grasped vainly at nothing as she was jostled from side to side. With great effort she made it up onto all fours, then tried to squat like the men around her. They smiled at her attempt before she was thrown into a pile of backpacks. Undeterred, she tried again, balancing like a surfer. Maddy's legs trembled with exhaustion as she mentally worked on the timing of her spectacular leap.

The bus rocked hard toward the inside of the track and then harder to the outside. Maddy was again thrown down on the metal roof. This time, two men grasped a leg and arm and pressed her down. She shrieked as the bus teetered on the edge of a roll.

"Holy shit, we're going over," she yelled, trying to scramble up and jump. But the men held her in place as they hung onto to the small roof rack. They did not speak but kept a firm grasp on her until the bus passed through the worst of the rocking ruts and came to a stop. The driver hung his head out the window and yelled in English: "Down now, too much danger." This time he was not negotiating.

By then Maddy was shaking and exhausted. She relented and was lowered to the ground. Richard smirked at her when she entered the cabin and she glared daggers at him. She pushed to the back and squeezed into a small space. There were no other alternatives. She accepted her impending doom with the rest of the riders, and fell asleep in a crash position.

The first few days of trekking were filled with awe during the day and agony at night. Lowland humid air gave rise to brilliant flowering rhododendrons that grew as large as trees. Marijuana plants grew wild and formed huge bushes that burst forth with dusty plumes. Richard led the trek along the winding Kali Gandaki River that climbed in gentle curves. Short bits of steep trail gave way to wider flats. The initial gradual slopes and low altitude made for fast walking and they covered over ten miles each day. At night after walking all day, Maddy gingerly removed her boots. In the quiet of the tiny teahouse lodge she whimpered and cradled her battered feet.

She had known that trekking would be arduous but never imagined her feet could hurt this much. Back home she had trained, hiking progressively more demanding terrain, but only one day at a time. Back to back days were different. Now, she stared at the dusty instruments of torture that rested in the corner. At early dawn, she coaxed her boots over swollen feet and took those first few painful steps of the day. By sun up her feet had softened. Thankfully, each day she grew stronger and became more adept at lifting her twenty kilo backpack until she was able to squat down with her pack on to drag a sweaty hand in an icy stream.

Richard was aloof and winced when the sun bounced off Maddy's still orange hair. They talked little, mostly to make walking plans for the day or discuss gear. Richard walked ahead and kept to himself except when he struck up a conversation with another trekker. When engaged by someone other than Maddy he would bloom like a spring flower at the opportunity to talk about himself or tell travel stories. Maddy observed this transformation again and again. How had they deteriorated so much just when they had reached the place that was supposed to heal them? Nepal was supposed to take away their stress, was supposed to capture and captivate them, to heal and repair their marriage.

The sights along each day's hike helped distract Maddy from disappointment. Long mule trains carried bulging loads up and down the trails supplying guesthouses and trekkers with food and goods including Coca Cola, Snickers, and English biscuits. Nepalis, having enjoyed or endured tourism since Sir Edmond Hilary and Tenzing Norgay reached the summit of Everest in 1953, understood that westerners loved a taste of home. Sherpas made a business of hauling goods up to the highest elevations. Sometimes they hauled products in baskets, but large deliveries were made by guided pack mules. The jingle of mule bells could be heard long before the trail-occupying train came into view.

In a narrow spot of track, Maddy converged with a long line of mules wearing bulbous saddle bags. She stepped to the outside of the trail on a small ledge to let them by. Several animals brushed her as they passed, their backs covered in brightly woven blankets of pinks and reds. The mules had dark eyes edged with long spidery lashes that made them look sleepy as they trod under their heavy loads. Maddy was so busy admiring their eyes that she failed to see the final mule in the train. He was huge, with wide bags that consumed the entire width of the trail. As he passed, he swayed and bumped her, pushing her to the far outside of the trail.

It only took one tiny step to be right on the edge, and she knew in an instant that she was too close. Maddy tipped backward slightly and began to lose her balance; the weight of her pack made it difficult to right herself. In slow motion her arms began to spin in tiny circles then larger twirls in a valiant balance-recovery effort. She began to fall backward off the ledge and could see her mother's face. Caroline had worried that Maddy could die while trekking. Maddy had dismissed this as a silly motherly fear. Now, the distinct possibility flashed through her mind. She slowly tipped beyond the point of recovery. Just before she fell, a young Nepali man came around the backside of the last mule and caught sight of the terror on Maddy's face. He took one swift step and grabbed a loose strap flailing from her pack and yanked her forward onto the trail. Maddy gasped for air and fell into the solid earth, her joints suddenly aching from the flood of adrenalin. The young man knelt down next to her as she gulped for air.

"Madam, please," he said. His voice was soft and kind. "Always on the inside." He patted her pack, then walked on quickly to catch up with the jingling mules; his flip flops added a soft tapping percussion to their song.

The trail narrowed quickly on the fifth day and clung to a rocky face that went up from the river valley with a steep rise. The scent of smoky fires filled the air as sleepy villages stirred to life. Maddy stopped for hot lemon tea to catch her breath as the elevation rose. The uphill sections were fierce but always rewarded with views down the valley or a cozy village built into the mountain side.

Maddy rounded a corner and was surrounded by a band of smiling children on their way to school. They were chirpy, with books tucked under arms, and called out 'Namaste.' Thick yak hair sweaters made the children look twice their natural girth. A girl with a blue dress and giant woolen mittens walked next to Maddy and grinned.

"You speak English?" Maddy asked.

The girl's cheeks widened into a smile but she did not reply. Maddy dug deep into memory to recall a few Nepali words.

"Koto janne?" Maddy asked the girl if she was going to Koto. Trying out her few words of Nepali made her smile.

The girl laughed, nodded to Maddy and then ran to catch up with her friends. They fell together giggling and whispering in a cluster. Maddy waved to the children as they scampered off. She mused at how incredible it must be to walk through the Himalayas each day to get to school.

Nepalese haulers went by carrying huge loads on thin head straps; eggs in paper crates stacked three feet high, and drums of cooking oil were carted up the trail. Men passed carrying four-by-fours to a construction site high above. Maddy watched in awe at the strength and grace of these nimble Nepali men who embodied a resourceful perseverance.

Farther up the trail, Richard struck up a conversation

with a Dutch couple. Idle travel chatter quickly turned to politics and travel ethics. They discussed the huge electric project under consideration which would bring power up to the small villages in the Annapurna region. Its scope was massive and would change daily life dramatically for locals and tourists alike. The topic had been hotly debated around the evening table the night before as to whether tourists would still come if the trekking experience became more modern. The 'third world' experience was a major reason that people flocked to Nepal from all over the world; the pureness of the Himalayas. The power project would require more roads into the mountain region and would forever change the trekking. Maddy loved the intellectual discourse and camaraderie of these conversations that evoked strong cultural, environmental, and social opinions. She pushed to keep up with Richard to better hear the conversation. But despite her improved strength, the pace was too fast and she knew that in a short time, he would be completely out of sight.

Initially she hadn't minded Richard's forging ahead while they were at lower elevations, but now that they were climbing steadily each day, she started to worry. Sometimes the trail would fork and she couldn't be sure which direction he had chosen. Other moments she felt that she might not want to walk as far as they had discussed, but once he was out of sight, there was no way to revise the plan. Maddy felt the uncomfortable paradox of needing him, while also wishing she didn't. She needed to break the habit of him, but he afforded her a level of security. The idea of trekking alone in this part of the world was daunting. There were always other people to walk with, but no one who would really look out for her in the event of an illness or injury. Her mind flashed back to when he'd left her alone in Egypt. If he didn't care then, why would he care now? Even still, the next morning Maddy asked Richard to wait for her mid-day just to make sure they didn't get too far apart. Richard just rolled his eyes at the suggestion.

Near Pisang, Maddy made her way up a steep portion of trail in the late afternoon and was surprised to see Richard waiting at a junction, his pack rested on the haulers wall. It was not the place at which they had agreed to meet so she was wary of him. Richard watched her come up the path and shook his head at her multi-colored gear; purple backpack, tan hiking shorts with zip off legs, grey tee-shirt, green gaiters, and two bandanas-- one pink, one blue--that hung like flags from her pack. She was out of breath when she reached him at the trail plateau.

"What's up?" She asked.

"I want to stay somewhere different tonight," he said. "Manang is going to be crowded."

"Ok. Where?"

He pointed up. "Garyu."

"How far up?" Maddy asked.

"About another hour walk." he replied.

Maddy sighed and dropped her head. At least he had

waited for her. "Alright," she said.

Richard slid his pack on and started up the dry zigzag path. Maddy tried to stay with him but soon fell behind as the trail ascended in sharp switchbacks. "Step-step-breathe," she repeated to herself as the air became thinner and her legs complained under the weight of her pack. Step-step-breathe. The trail climbed up and up until Richard was just a tiny dot moving on a thin pencil line of terrain. Maddy scanned for the village high above but could only see a narrow break in the rocky relief that was too small to be inhabited. As she huffed along, Maddy tried to calculate the distance and time it would take her to get to the top. With each step she became more and more angry. There was no way she would reach Garyu before the sun went down. What a stupid idea this was! Why had she agreed to climb so high after a full day of elevation gain already? Fury swelled red hot inside her contrasting against the cooling air. She looked down and contemplated turning back, leaving Richard to his ridiculous climb. Sadly she realized she was carrying all their money and could not bear the idea that a poor host family would not get paid for his food and lodging because she had refused to climb. Crap. Maddy stomped her feet and tried to spit but her tongue was too dry. She trudged up the rocky trail.

The sun was down when she reached the final switchback that opened onto a wider path at the base of Gyaru. Richard strolled toward her in the shadowy night.

"This is not a village," Maddy fired. "There are only

three houses."

"I got us a room," he said.

Using the last bit of rage-fueled strength in her legs, Maddy strode past him. He had to turn and jog to catch her, then he led her to a narrow wooden two-story guesthouse. The first level, occupied by the host family, consisted of a low single room blackened from a makeshift stove that inhabited the center of the floor. A pile of yak rugs served as a bed for the two adults and two children who lived at this crazy-high elevation. A crate of eggs, bags of rice and lentils and a stack of darkened cooking pots were stored on shelves along the back wall. A slight man with a wide Tibetan forehead tended a smoky fire and smiled when Maddy arrived.

"Room upstairs, Madam." He gestured toward a narrow staircase. Please, not more elevation. She smiled and nodded in thanks. The stairs creaked up to a loft of exposed timber. Slanted beams created a high point in the roofline such that it was only possible to stand in the center of the room. The floor was covered with a layer of straw. Sleeping platforms were made from small bails of straw laid side by side and tucked under the eaves. Richard had spread his orange mummy bag out over a straw bed on the far end of the room. Maddy dropped her gear by a bed adjacent to a window; the night was turning from blue to black.

"Where's the bathroom?" Maddy asked.

Richard's face pulled into a smirk and he pointed toward the stairs. Maddy hobbled down the staircase to find the small sooty man in the kitchen.

"Kaksha kahaan cha?" she tried. The man beamed at her linguistic effort and motioned for her to follow. He went out the kitchen door and turned sharply around the back into a tiny alley. He must share a bathroom with his neighbor. She followed him past the next house and continued out onto the main path. He stopped and pointed up the tiny line of houses. "Please no," Maddy whispered and looked back to the man who waved at her with a flick of his wrist.

"Thank you," she said quietly. Her shoulders slumped. A one-hundred yard walk to the community outhouse was fine during the day, but not at night, and not at this elevation. Sleeping at altitude required great volumes of water to avoid dehydration. Altitude=hydration=bathroom. As she plodded up the trail she wondered if maybe Richard was trying to kill her.

After washing up in a tiny basin Maddy joined the smoky family for a bowl of dahl baht--lentils and rice, cooked long and slow. It was accompanied by a cup of dark earthy tea. The children sang Nepalese songs and danced to pass the evening. One more trudge to the outhouse left Maddy winded with altitude. Finally, she climbed into her sleeping bag and tried to sleep, but none came. Her heart was still beating fast from the trip to the bathroom- surely it would quiet down soon. But her pulse beat rapid and thready and only worsened as she worried. Tachycardia was one of the early signs of altitude sickness, when the heart pumps fast and hard to circulate the miniscule amount of oxygen available. Maddy flipped on her headlamp and searched her Guide to Nepal. She located the Annapurna circuit and found a description of Gyaru: four thousand meters- just over thirteen thousand feet.

"What if I die up here?" Maddy said aloud into the darkness.

She had heard stories from other trekkers about people who started with a simple headache and pounding heart and ended up with cerebral edema, only to be carried down unconscious, on the back of a mule, limbs flopping with each step. She checked her pulse again. It seemed to be stuck at one hundred and thirty-five, which also seemed to be the temperature inside her sleeping bag. She kicked out of the down bag in an anxious sweat and guzzled a half bottle of water, which only made her have to go to the bathroom again.

On the way back from the outhouse, her mind rambled to dark places and she wondered what would happen to her body if she died at thirteen thousand feet. Would Richard have her buried in a mountainous stone grave? Would he try to take her back down? Would he grieve? She shook her head at the irony. She had imagined him dead several times lately but perhaps she was the one in jeopardy.

She must have finally slept, for when she woke, the clouds had cleared. Outside the small window the moon showed brightly in the black night. It illuminated the snow crested peak of Annapurna I--the largest of the sister peaks. Maddy crawled to the low window and pressed close.

The mountain seemed only inches away. Its immense presence filled the view. Velvety white snow rippled over the mountain face and folded into deep shadowy crevasses. Maddy's heart raced. She crept back to bed and lay in silent reverence for a long time before falling back asleep.

In the morning, while the light was still grey and filled with early fog, she got up quietly and packed her bag. She gratefully accepted a cup of hot tea and a bowl of pasty porridge in the kitchen. The guest house was quiet. She paid the keeper in folded rupee notes and left through the small door. The path was covered in frost. It gave off a ghostly sheen. At the edge of Gyaru, Maddy stopped and looked up where Annapurna had shown in the night. Now, there were only dense clouds against a dark sky. She smiled and held the memory close. She had been gifted a private showing of the sacred peak. She walked slowly and savored the privilege of having seen its beauty. On the edge of town she ran her hand along the row of prayer wheels, giving thanks to the universe.

Seven

Richard caught up with Maddy at the edge of Manang. "Why did you leave so early?" He asked. The sun was just up and had barely unthawed the trail.

"Why do you care?" She said.

He looked at her, slightly wounded, bags collected around his eyes. "Well, you could have waited for me," Richard said.

"I could have waited? I could have waited!" Her voice echoed in the morning air with a pierce of disbelief. She sputtered, cheeks flushed. "Oh for fuck's sake." Maddy pushed past Richard and stomped toward the opening shops.

Manang rested at the mouth of the trekking ascent and had become the preparation spot where travelers pooled to rest, repack, restock, and learn. From there it was only two more days walk before hiking up and over Thorong La, the eighteen thousand foot pass. It was a bustling village full of guides and trekkers. Manang was the village that Frederick had mentioned and the guide book recommended several days stay to allow for altitude acclimatization.

Two western doctors, who had watched too many trekkers come down with altitude sickness, had established a clinic that offered first aid classes on how to spot the signs of high altitude illness. They also took donations of unused medications and re-prescribed them to sick locals and travelers. Remembering Frederick's advice, she signed up for a class the next day and went to find a place to relax away from Richard.

But he had a knack for finding Maddy during meal times and he dropped down next to her for lunch. She tried to ignore him but was again caught in a dilemma. She knew it was not safe for her to cross the pass alone and it was too late to hire a guide. He sat beside her at a tea house table and ordered vegetable fried noodles and a beer.

"Seriously, you are going to have a beer at fifteen thousand feet?" Maddy shook her head.

"What?" He shrugged.

"Aren't you going to hike the training peak this afternoon?" Maddy asked.

"No, I don't feel like hiking it today," Richard said.

Maddy nodded, trying not to show her disappointment. "Here, take some rupees so you can eat where you want and don't have to find me every meal." She slid a stack of bills across the table.

"Whatever," Richard said, taking the money. He ate and drank in silence.

After lunch, Maddy wandered the narrow trails that traced the mountain side like a spider web. The sun was high and its heat was just enough to counteract the cool mountain air. Himalayan peaks created spectacular views all around. A group of trekkers, resting their legs for the impending climb, had gathered in a cluster on the trail where a crude wooden bench had been built. It was a perfect place to sit in the sun. But as Maddy approached, she saw Richard on the bench. A few feet away a yak, covered in hair so long it looked as if it wore a poncho, stepped from the grassy area onto the trail. The yak had likely come over the pass led by a Tibetan trader who had stopped in Manang for a meal. The bell around the yak's neck swung slowly with the wide shuffle of his gait. He snuffled at the ground and ambled toward the bench. As the yak approached the resting spot, several people hopped up and sprinted away leaving Richard the sole occupant.

Richard sat with his legs stretched out onto the trail, his head back and eyes closed. He had fallen asleep. Maddy, now twenty yards away, watched the mountainous yak lumber up to the bench and sniff the air. Her heart raced as the animal lifted his head up and down. Thick calloused horns tapered into sharp points.

"Holy crap," Maddy mumbled as the yak lowered his head toward Richard. If she did nothing, just watched, he could be gored right there. She hadn't imagined this as a possible way for Richard to go.

The yak took one step closer and Maddy squeaked, "Richard."

He jolted awake and gasped at seeing the great animal

before him. His sudden movement startled the yak, who jerked away and off the track. Richard looked up at Maddy and she gave a small wave. Her heartbeat filled her ears.

Maddy kept to herself on the final rest day in Manang and avoided Richard whenever possible. She wasn't exactly alone, for he was always on the periphery, but she enjoyed the freedom of sitting with a German couple for dinner or striking up conversation with an Israeli woman who sat for hours to study her map. When the sun went down, Maddy returned to their room and found Richard going through his pack. She could tell that he was antsy to get moving again.

"I want to leave early tomorrow for Thorong Phedi. I'll just meet you there if you want to sleep in," Richard said as Maddy went to bed.

"It would be safer if we stayed together for the next several days," she said. "Just in case of altitude sickness."

"You'll be fine," he said. "Besides, I want to get there early and get us a room. I hear it can get crowded if the conditions are poor—trekkers back up for days."

"Ok, then I'll get up and walk with you." Maddy said. She pulled her sleeping bag up over her head and fell asleep.

Richard was gone when Maddy woke in the morning. She fumed at his leaving, especially since she had specifically asked him to walk with her. She grabbed a quick breakfast and headed out alone for the long uphill trek to the last village before the pass.

Thorong Phedi emerged from the clouds after six hours of vigorous hiking. It was a small village at nearly seventeen thousand feet perched on the side of Annapurna. Gone were the relative comforts of lower elevation. Here, everything was about getting up and over the pass. Trekkers piled into big dormitory-style rooms. The guesthouse was crowded but Maddy saw Richard when she came in breathing heavily. She sat down to rest at a long table where the weather was being discussed at great length like a meteorologist convention.

"Three AM is ideal," offered an angular German man with the face of a collie. "Best to get on the trail before it gets busy and before the clouds gather."

"It's too dark then," replied his Swiss companion.

Maddy interrupted. "Why leave so early if it's not that high of a climb--only a thousand more feet from where we are now?"

"Yes, not a big elevation gain, but the effort required at this altitude is much greater, making it a very slow climb; approximately twelve hours up and over," the German man said.

"And the altitude can make you confused a bit. Be sure not to go alone." Both men nodded.

Maddy looked around to see if Richard was in earshot to hear this. Suddenly she was nervous and wanted to talk to him. Would he be arrogant enough to leave her behind again tomorrow? What if she got sick and delirious and could not get over the pass? This summit was not like Everest, but high enough to cause problems. She had to find Richard and talk to him. The dorm was like a hurricane shelter with cots and gear and people and sweat. Maddy found Richard in a far corner and startled him with her urgent voice.

"We have to stay together tomorrow. What time do you want to leave?"

"Around four thirty," he said. "The kitchen said they would have tea ready then."

"Don't leave without me," she said. "I mean it." She found an empty cot one row down and sifted through her gear to prepare for the early morning ahead.

No one slept well among the snoring and farting of too many bodies pressed into the space and once the first person stirred, everyone got up. People bumped around in the darkness in search of their boots. The kitchen came to life and people cued up, praying for warm tea. Maddy pulled her hat farther down over her ears and shivered. She had been wearing the hat for at least a week and her hair was a tangled mess, every follicle tender from the continuous pressure and matting. She coaxed herself up and put on layers of clothes: long johns, polypropylene pants, and a fleece jacket covered by a wind shell. Richard came over and gave a grizzled nod toward the kitchen. They stood in line for some porridge and a cup of tea, stamping their feet to pound life into their icy cold boots.

Small groups departed through the side door into the darkness. Maddy breathed deep and tried to quiet her nervous stomach and kept an eye on Richard for signs of departure. She got up to get another cup of tea and to pay for their lodging and meals. She returned to the table and stared at the empty spot on the bench where Richard had been.

"You've got to be kidding," Maddy said. She scanned the room but could not find Richard in the dim light. She handed her cup to a sleepy woman in the tea line. "Here, it's hot--I have to go."

Maddy heaved her pack over her shoulders stepped out into the inky morning. The only light came from the small bulbs on headlamps of trekkers up ahead, forming a ghostly dot-to-dot in the shifting fog. She walked as quickly as she could manage in the dark and at elevation. She spoke "Namaste" softly as she came upon and passed hikers. She scanned for Richard's face in hopes of catching him before the big ascent. With each step she grew angrier at his audacity and complete self-centeredness. She gained a small measure of pleasure at the idea of him facing her mother to explain how he had left Maddy to hike and die alone in the Himalayas. He would deserve Caroline's wrath.

The light came up slowly around six thirty and the trail turned from mud to slush to snow and narrowed into a thin single-file track. With better light she could see further and spotted Richard several hundred yards ahead moving slowly and being passed on the trail. Eager to catch him and fueled by fury, Maddy made good time and caught up to Richard just at the foot of the steep incline where he had stopped to rest. He was breathing heavily in the thin air and leaned on his knees. He looked as if he was snapping at the waning molecules of air. The sky was clear and pale blue-grey with light coming from below, illuminating the edges of the mountain. Maddy looked ahead at a giant snow field that swept up along the vertical expanse of the mountain's face. An ant trail of trekkers dotted the mountainside in a continuous line through the white carpet of snow. Maddy stepped past Richard but faced away from him not wanting to look at his face.

"Why didn't you wait for me?" She asked.

He glanced at her and shrugged unable to catch his breath or unwilling to answer.

"I'm leaving you." Maddy said with sudden clarity. She moved forward on strong legs: Step-Step-Breathe, Step-Step-Breathe. Despite the thin air she felt good. She breathed in rhythm and moved up the mountain.

"Maddy," came his hoarse breathy voice from behind her. "Maddy wait," Richard called.

She stopped and breathed slowly as a tidal wave of anger washed over her. Its intensity made her dizzy and she tipped slightly on the incline. She looked down to steady her feet. The snow was up to her shins.

"Wait?" She turned toward him with black steel eyes.

"Please wait for me," he said in a breathless voice.

Maddy closed her eyes to calm the storm in her head. She recalled being sick and delirious in Egypt. She remembered the previous weeks of walking alone. She noted how he bolted each day and rarely checked in with her until evening. Now he wanted her to wait?

"Why should I wait for you now?" Spittle flew from her curled lips.

"I can't make it over without help, I can hardly breathe." Richard rasped.

"So suddenly, you need me?" Maddy yelled. The words skipped off the snow and pelted Richard below.

"Please," he mouthed.

Maddy hung her head. She stood still and stared at the snow. She had visualized his death many times, but now when faced directly with the choice of leaving him on the mountain, she paused. What kind of person was she? What kind of person did she want to be? She stood glacially still. Maddy remembered how helpless she had been when she was sick. She remembered how kind Jack had been about caring for her. Jack has been a stranger and still he had shown her compassion. She wanted to be better than the person she had become in her marriage. She didn't want to be angry or hateful. The grace of Annapurna grounded her, surrounded her with quiet, and evoked compassion. She could not leave him there. She didn't want him to die. Despite all their difficulties, her anger, his egocentricity, she knew she could not leave him there.

Finally, she nodded toward Richard and stepped down

116

to him. He labored to extract oxygen from the attenuated air. Maddy gave him sips of water and small bites of Snickers for energy. He went slowly and she coached him in the Step-Step-Breathe rhythm she had read about in the hikers' guide. Together, they climbed toward the summit.

The sky was gargantuan at Thorong La and strings of weathered prayer flags flapped like laundry. Richard and Maddy stopped long enough for a brief photo. Relief and excitement was mixed with sadness. Even summiting the 18,000 foot pass could not displace the void in her heart. She knew the marriage was going to end. Her naïve idea of healing was gone. She stepped away from the main trail for a moment beyond the battered flags. The mountain had a power all its own. It spoke of wisdom and a strange combination of steadfastness and continual change. Its actual peak high above, revealed greater places still, and Maddy saw that this crossing was just a false height. If she were a true climber she would face more mountain above, more struggle, and more reward. But she was here and had reached the place that she never really believed was possible. The air was so thin at 18,000 feet she knew it was not safe to stay long; they needed to get down to better oxygen. She bent low to help Richard tighten his boots and they set out for the descent.

Maddy kept a steady downhill pace. With each step toward a lower altitude, Richard felt better. They descended quickly, so quickly that she was struck by sharp spikes of pain that filled her head and settled in behind her eyes.

Each thudding step vibrated her brain and she winced with a post-altitude headache. She downed Ibuprofen and Tylenol like M&M's. Richard stayed near and silent and watched Maddy squint and squeeze her temples until they finally stopped for lunch and rest. She took her boots off and lay back on a rocky slope to rest and wait for a bowl of rice. Trekkers passed sporting huge smiles at making it over the pass. One man clicked by with lean trekking poles; his speed and fluidity looked effortless. He nodded as he passed and Maddy watched him glide over the trail until he was out of sight. After a bit of food, she garnered the strength to pull on her boots and made the final descent into Muktinah.

By the end of the walk, her feet were numb, just blocks of wood encapsulated by dirt-encrusted leather. The guesthouse host was accustomed to trekkers coming in battered and beaten. Maddy took a bucket of hot water and bathed, washed clothes, and soaked her feet. She hung her shirts on the line and then joined a small group at the dining table. Everyone was tired and groaned audibly when lowering to sit, everyone except for Franz--the blond Austrian who had clicked past Maddy with terrific speed earlier that day; he moved with ease. He was fit and had been hiking all over the Himalayas for months. His body was sinewy as a long-distance runner and he raked his hand through his just washed spiky hair.

"Made it up and over," he chided in a friendly tone as she sat down.

"Indeed." Maddy hoped she was mirroring the nonchalant confidence he exuded. He laughed, making her smile honestly for the first time in weeks.

"Some tea will help you recover." He poured hot, lemony liquid into a cup. It steamed golden and bright.

"Do the trekking poles help?" she inquired, seeking some rationale for his amazing speed.

"Certainly, I never climb without them." Franz's blue eyes held captured energy like a deep well.

"Maybe I'll get some poles to try on the way down." It had taken eleven days of vigorous walking to get to the pass, many long downhill days loomed ahead.

"You can try mine if you like." His accent was direct and inviting.

"Um, sure, ok. That would be great." Maddy said, not sure what type of invitation he offered. Surely he did not expect her to take the sticks for a spin this evening, she could barely walk.

Reading her mind, he laughed. "Not tonight. Tomorrow, or whenever you head out."

"You want to walk with us when we go?" She questioned in disbelief. Hadn't he seen her hobbling? There was no way he would want to go at her pace.

"I'll go with you, and you can see if the poles make a difference." He winked.

A feeling Maddy had not had in many years flipped like a trampoline gymnast in her stomach.

"Sounds great," she said with a bit too much enthusiasm. He laughed again then rose to get more tea.

She pretended to write in her travel journal and kept her head down to hide a smile. Maddy was elated by Franz's attention and at the idea that she might still be desirable after such a deep winter of a marriage. Before Richard, she had always enjoyed the playful banter of a fun relationship; spontaneous sexual romps and the exchange of compliments and laughter. But these were distant memories that had not stirred until now. She was tugged by the profound urge to flee the invisible constraints of marriage. Had she actually told Richard that she was leaving in such a way that he understood it to be true? Had she meant it?

Maddy slept restlessly and waited with anticipation for morning. Breakfast was early and she was up, bathed, and ready to go. Nervously giddy, Maddy sat at the table full of travelers inhaling the aroma of fresh mint tea. Richard sat beside her, nursing a cup of coffee. Her heart pounded as she mustered a false casual voice.

"I'm going to take off early and try out Franz's trekking poles." Richard barely looked up from the steaming cup as Maddy slid some Nepalese Rupee over to him. "Here's some money in case we don't meet up."

"Do you still want to stay in Marpha tonight?" He asked.

Franz sat down just then. "Marpha is great," he said. "You can get chocolate strudel and carrot cake there. A Swiss woman and her husband run the famous Bakery

Guesthouse."

"Sounds great," Maddy replied. She was not sure if Richard realized she was leaving with Franz. She got up and grabbed her pack before he could connect the dots.

"See you later." Maddy said and zipped out the door grabbing the trekking poles off Franz's pack. Her heart raced as she tasted freedom. She was drunk on adrenalin and walked with tremendous speed enjoying the clicking rhythm of the poles on the rocky trail.

"Nice pace," came Franz's smooth voice a few steps behind. "Think you can keep it up?"

"For at least ten minutes," she called back. It felt good to be moving.

Franz smiled as he caught up and easily maintained her speed. "What's your plan?" he asked.

"No idea." Maddy glanced at him. "It's like a jail break, once you're out, not sure what to do."

"You should have seen the confusion on his face." Franz said of Richard.

A giddy laugh escaped Maddy's throat and the sound carried out into the valley. The trail got wider and wider and became a huge scooping path that yawned into an enormous sand flat. It was a dry river bed with small grey rocks embroidered into the sand and spread out for a hundred feet on each side. It was vast and windswept and completely unprotected. The sand began to swirl into dusty clouds and Franz stopped to dig out his sunglasses. Maddy wrapped a pink bandana over her nose and mouth like a bandit in hope of keeping the sand out of her teeth. The light conversation they had been holding came to a close as they turned into the wind. Franz tapped her shoulder and pointed to a rock outcropping down the valley. Maddy nodded and they took off.

Wind and sand pelted sharply as they traversed the slope. It was slow going and Maddy's eyes were filled with sand when they reached the rocky shelf and ducked behind. She caught her breath and welcomed the quiet afforded by the shielding rocks. The space was very tight and they huddled close together. Eventually, his accented voice brought the question she'd feared all morning.

"You're having trouble with your husband?"

Replying "no" would have been utterly ridiculous. She had hiked all day with a virtual stranger and was happily squished into a wind cave next to the first man who had nudged a toe into the door of her crumbling marital facade. She sifted sand into a small pile by her feet.

"Yes, It's been bad the whole trip, and before that too." Maddy stated numbly. "Have you ever been married?"

"Yes, many years ago. We were very different."

"Is that how you ended up in Nepal--the end of the relationship?" She asked.

"I've always traveled, but for shorter periods," he explained. "After we split up there was really nothing to keep me home. I love it here; I can walk forever."

"Are you avoiding going home?" Maddy felt suddenly brazen and intimate.

122

"Probably," he said after a pause. "I love the freedom of trekking, the beauty of the mountains and meeting new people." He reached out and gently squeezed her arm. Maddy swallowed hard and looked at his hand. She wanted desperately to touch him back; it had been an excruciatingly long time. She dragged her fingers in the sand. The tiny sand crystals embraced diverse hues of grey, tan, and sable. They gave way under her fingers, creating smooth furrows, warm on the surface and cooler in the darker, underneath layer. She slowly brushed over the grooves with a careful sliding hand to restore the continuous surface that looked solid on upon initial inspection, but shifted easily with the lightest force.

Maddy gently picked up his hand and held it between hers, resting her forehead on this tripod. Eyes closed, she could hear her heart beating, aware of the liminal boundary on which she teetered. The wind was constant and he remained still. His hand was cool and dry in her damp grip and she slid it down to her lips. His fingers were lightly rough and salt scented.

"Let's walk." Maddy uttered almost imperceptibly. He smiled and brushed her cheek tenderly, then stood and helped her up. Her pack felt a hundred stone and she was compressed between its weight and the pressure of the wind. Franz offered her the poles.

"You were doing quite well with these," he smiled.

They moved with little speed and even less conversation down the open valley toward Marpha.

Eight

Chocolate strudel oozed over the pan as it left the stove. The Bakery Guesthouse was packed with trekkers relishing exotic baked treats. The dark-haired hostess pushed moist curls away from her face and sliced thick rounds of cinnamon bread; the scent of cinnamon permeated the room. Maddy ate lemon Bundt cake and sipped on a cup of dark, sweet coffee while Franz sat near reading his book. He had a comfortable presence without expectation, like a melody playing in the background.

Richard arrived near sunset and was indifferent to Maddy but pleased to find a bottle of Gorka beer. After a brief exchange, they ignored each other. The tables were now crowded and opinionated international conversations filled the air. Britain's lease on Hong Kong had expired earlier that year and diverse viewpoints on Chinese culture and policy were offered up for debate. A Dutch traveler suggested that China replace its one-child policy with free televisions. Maddy laughed too loud in agreement; TV had certainly curbed the sex life for many western couples.

With a full stomach and tired legs, Maddy was eager for sleep. She gave Richard a room number and got up to leave. She wanted to speak with Franz, to thank him for a great day, the use of his trekking poles, and for awakening in her a latent desire, but he was deep in conversation. As she got to the stairs Maddy swept her gaze toward him one more time. He caught her eyes and smiled with a gentle nod as if tipping a hat. She placed her hands together with a tiny bow of the head and mouthed Namaste, and went off to bed.

Maddy woke to Richard's snoring and the smell of apple fritters fresh from the oven. She marveled again at how all the delectable treats could be produced in such a primitive kitchen. She dressed, went down for breakfast, and scanned the room eagerly for Franz.

"He already left," came the Dutch inflection.

Maddy deflated. She nodded and plopped down on the bench.

"Were you traveling together?" he asked.

"Just briefly."

The Dutchman poured her a cup of tea and she lowered her face over the steam. It was minty and moistened her eyes. Small leaves floated in the bronze current drifting and turning. She dropped in an irregular lump of sugar and watched the crystals disintegrate. Maddy envisioned Franz gracefully navigating the rocky downhill terrain with his poles keeping him perfectly balanced. It had been just one day; the door of opportunity nudged open ever so slightly, yet the internal shift was much greater; she loathed the return to indifference, irrelevance.

Many table mates sat, ate, and left as she slumped over her tea, the steam long gone. Eventually, Richard was next to her and slid the Annapurna map over and jabbed a finger toward Tatopani. Not knowing what else to do, she nodded, abandoned her tea and took her pack out the door. As they descended, the humidity rose. It filled the air with heavy, moist clouds that hung low on the trail before bursting forth in a heave of rain. Rivulets of water traversed down into groves made by repetitive flows until the trickle became introverted under foliage. In Tatopani, the rain became thick and Maddy refused to walk on the slick stone trail. For days, the valley foliage dripped in green emeralds. Maddy holed up in the window seat of a quaint guesthouse with a library. She gloomily perused books, wore her long johns all day, drank tea, and slept.

Occasionally, Richard poked his head into the small room, but mostly left her alone. After several days, the rain let up and he became restless to move on. Richard creaked open the small wooden library door and ducked into the book filled room. The natural light from the far-end window had drained away an hour before. Maddy huddled on the window seat using her headlamp to read. Richard sat down across the room and waited for her to look up.

"Maddy," he said softly. "We need to leave tomorrow. There is a break in the rain, the trail should be good."

She stared in his direction barely recognizing the man she had married. He was happy once, smiling and laughing, but now he looked weathered and sullen. She took a breath and asked the question that should have been asked years ago.

"What are we doing? Why are we staying together?"

He slumped further into the worn chair.

"We're both miserable and we haven't had sex in forever." Maddy said.

Richard cringed at this truth. Now out in the open air it hung there, took up residence, crowding the room and pushing back the novels and travel guides that lined the shelves.

"I don't know," Richard said. "I don't know how to fix it."

He spoke as if their relationship were carpentry; a broken hutch, one leg cracked and drawers that no longer closed or opened properly. Neither Gorilla Glue nor hardware could reconstitute the broken bond. Maddy turned toward the dark window and cried.

"Maddy," he said, "we can't make this decision here, in the mountains of Nepal. Let's get down to Pokhara where we can warm up and take a shower and think."

She wiped her eyes and nodded. He followed her back to the room and they began to pack.

The sun perched high over the lake side city and the majestic peak called Fish Tail Mountain filled the blue canvas sky. The sacred mountain loomed over the city like a skyscraper and could be seen from anywhere in town. It was both a shock and relief to Maddy to be off the Annapurna trail and out of the mountains after so many weeks. Cars sputtered and puffed out dark smoke, dodging cows that filled the streets.

Maddy and Richard found a quaint guesthouse that overlooked Lake Pokhara. It had pathways adorned by bright flowers. Maddy sat at the outdoor table and wrote postcards to friends and family. She tapped her pen on her lips as she considered what to write: amazed, sad, overstimulated, underweight, lost. After several attempts, she quit trying to capture the paradox and just wrote: The mountains are brilliant. Wish you were here. There was no way to convey the mixed up state of her life. It seemed ridiculous to be on this once-in-a-lifetime trip, and all the while knowing her marriage was crumbling.

She and Richard had spoken little on the last two days of trekking before they emerged onto the steep mountain road and flagged down a ride into Pokhara. It hadn't helped that Maddy had caught a stomach bug and spent most of her non-trail time in the loo. She was exhausted from not sleeping well and from having to shoo away the small herd of pygmy goats that visited the bathroom all night. But now she was out of the mountains, showered and dressed in new, clean cotton pants and an Indian style tunic she bought from a local merchant.

Richard had left her alone all day. The sun was low and the air had begun to cool when he spied Maddy as she came in from the picnic table. He met her at a table in the common area. Richard stood close but did not sit down. He awkwardly produced a small paper-wrapped parcel and smiled--almost.

"It's your birthday soon," he said.

Maddy unwrapped the brown paper and unfolded the creases methodically, smoothing out each wrinkle. Inside was a pair of delicate silver loops onto which clung a deep blue lapis stone. They were beautiful and she offered a weak smile.

"Thank you," she said and turned the smooth silver in her hands. After a moment she slid over and Richard sat down. They sat as if waiting for a bus, knowing it was proper to talk to each other in such close proximity but neither wanting to go first. Maddy refolded the gift wrap until it was tiny and she slid it into her pocket.

"What do you want to do?" Richard asked.

"About the trip or about us?"

"Both I guess," he replied.

Maddy stared at the long wooden table that was worn and scarred; its grooves held history of plans and hope, laughter and stories, dirt and fatigue. Maddy liked the sturdiness of its base that didn't budge when leaned on.

"I do want to see India," she said.

"With me?"

Maddy sighed, "I don't know."

Richard ran a rough hand through his hair. "We are both

unhappy, that's a given, but I don't think you should travel alone in India. Let's go to India together and when we get back to Bangkok we can regroup."

Maddy pondered the proposal and wondered if it was a reprieve or a further sentence.

"Remember the couple we met at the beginning of Annapurna, Simon and Rose," he said. "I ran into them at the market. They are headed to India in a few days and asked if we wanted to meet up with them there."

Maddy brightened slightly at the idea of traveling with another couple; it would be a good diversion.

"Ok, that would be nice," she said.

It was like the close of a business deal and Maddy almost reached out to shake on it, but pulled back.

"Thank you for the earrings." she said.

Nine

The flight to Varanasi, called Banares by the locals, landed in the early morning and Maddy was immediately overtaken by the noise and chaos and smell. They disembarked the plane and were swept up in a crush that took them through customs, baggage, and then out onto the street, where throngs of merchants and drivers and hawkers and tuk-tuk's converged. The sounds were a cacophony of--"Baksheesh, Baksheesh"--"Pakora, Pakora, Pakora"-- "Chai! Chai! Chai!"

Maddy turned in the street and found a tiny clay cup thrust into her hands and looked at the thin dark man who said, "It is very sweet Madam, drink it, good chai." He gestured a drinking motion and Maddy followed the cue instinctively. The tea was cloudy, milky, and warm with a hint of cardamom. She fumbled in her pocket and gave him a crumpled bill, which was far too much money for one cup of tea. He beamed as if he'd won the lottery and bowed in thanks only to be swallowed up by the moving crowd.

The tuk-tuk driver putted along the maze of streets in the old city; the golf cart-like vessel weaved around people and cows and goats. Smoke puffed from two stroke engine motorcycles that whizzed past. The streets formed a complex network of intersecting alleys and busy thoroughfares lined by shops and beggars and monkeys and shrines and a host of unimaginable things. A cow decorated in beautiful robes came down the road led on a gold tether; skeletally thin men squatted in the streets holding copper bowls hoping for a few rupee donations; children crouched over a huge pan of bubbling yogurt. Everything was both a delight and an assault on the senses, mixing the sweet aroma of musky incense with the smells of decay.

They arrived at the Scindhia Hotel and checked into a stark room high above the Ganges River. Maddy dropped her pack and rifled around for the India travel guide she had traded for her Nepal book at the airport. Out on the balcony, she plopped into a chair to read about the ancient city. Varanasi was sacred because of its location on the Ganges River. Bathing, praying in, and even drinking the holy water was considered by many to be a spiritual event and a lifetime quest. Many Hindus across India made the pilgrimage to Varanasi in their final weeks or months of life in order to be cremated and have their ashes sprinkled into the river. Maddy leaned over the edge of the balcony to study the water. It looked like chocolate milk but not in a desirable way and it moved with a viscous quality. On the huge steps down into the water, holy men with long braided hair and dressed only in white cotton rags, sat in meditation. Other men waded out into the water to perform ritual dips and used tiny silver urns to pour water as their lips moved in silent prayer.

Further down and out into the current a group of teenage girls stood hip-deep talking and laughing with faces close; their brilliant white teeth flashed against creamy brown skin as they smiled. The bright colors of their saris deepened in the water bleeding crimson red and cerulean blue into the Ganges. Washer women beat clothing against rocks to release the suds before plunging the fabric back into the water to rinse.

Maddy read further that a family's wealth could be ascertained by the quality of the sari cloth and poorer women wore paler colors and fabric of limited weft. It was clear that the river played a central role in the lives of the people below, but Maddy could not get past the fact that the water was absolutely filthy. Despite her fatigue, she was fascinated and called to Richard, "Let's go have a look around."

They walked through the labyrinth of streets and turned away from the river. Out on the busy wide road scrawny children begged for money with outstretched hands. Ragged women sat against the walls hoping for food or money from passersby. To deny a child or starving man a few coins seemed cruel but the moment Maddy reached toward her pocket the mob of hands multiplied along with the chorus of requests. It was like being swarmed by bees, surrounded, no matter where she turned or stepped to try to gain space, people crushed in. Richard finally hollered: "Enough!" Maddy doubted that the children understood the word, but his tone was unmistakable.

They veered away from the main street and back toward the river and fell into a long procession of people who walked and chanted down a narrow corridor. The pulsing minor key song grew loud and tones of wailing and weeping were added like instruments of grief: a funeral procession. Up in front, a line of men in crisp sky blue shirts carried a tightly wrapped body bound to a stretcher of poles. The body was carried above the men's heads as though already ascending. The alleyway widened out at the river ghats, and the procession split into two groups; the pallbearers continued down to the burning platform and the other group stopped and formed a huddle. Maddy, caught in the current of people, stopped in the crowded circle. At the center and squatting on her haunches was a frail older woman, her yellow sari draping on the ground. Her head was held back, face pierced in grief. She sobbed audibly while a serious looking man stood over her with a straight blade and carefully shaved off long lengths of black hair. The locks mixed with tears and wept to the ground.

"Why?" Maddy whispered. "Why?"

The man next to her explained. "Her husband has died and she must shave her head in the Hindu tradition of mourning."

Maddy's breath caught mid-chest. She could feel the palpable loss of the shorn woman, her sorrow rolling off in waves. The family members helped the woman stand and enveloped her back into the procession that led down to the river.

Parts of the river walk were off limits to foot traffic, tourists, and cameras. The burning ghats, where bodies were cremated, would only allow those carrying the deceased. Cremations were carried out around the clock and Maddy and Richard inched closer to the steps to get a glimpse. An entrepreneurial man came forth and offered his services.

"I can take you out in my boat to see from the water," he said.

Richard looked at Maddy who nodded agreement.

"You may not take photos; that is disrespectful." The man clarified.

Richard agreed and they followed. His name was Naresh and he took on the role of both boatman and docent, sharing history and pointing out landmarks as he ferried them out into the river in a small rowboat. The view was phenomenal, a completely different perspective of river life. The banks were jammed with people, colors, fabric, flowers, bathers, mourners, hawkers and holy men, all connected by the sacred water. Maddy looked on as people dunked repeatedly as if in self-baptism while others brushed their teeth.

"It's is a sacred act to bathe in the Ganges," Naresh said. "To be washed of ten life times of sin." His deep brown eyes were lined with creases at the corners and squinted in time with his sing-song accent. "The people can only come during the dry season for when it rains the water rises." He pointed to a craggy high water mark on the building and Maddy imagined the brown mucky water overtaking the praying Sadhu's and chai fires.

"The river looks quite dirty," she said. "Do people worry about their health?"

Naresh looked at her, perplexed. His thick eyebrows furrowed together. "No worries, the Ganges is sacred." His head bobbed gently side to side as he spoke.

Thick sludge gathered in slow sections. Maddy tried again to clarify. "I understand that the water is considered sacred, but it is also dirty--yes?"

"Everything is ok, the Ganges is sacred." Naresh repeated as if stuck in a groove.

Maddy shrugged and looked at Richard who had his lens trained at the burning ghats.

"No photos of the cremation." Naresh said sternly.

"No, no," Richard replied. "I'm shooting the buildings on the hill."

Maddy knew that Richard had no scruples when it came to his photography. He would click away endlessly in temples or private weddings. Maddy was never comfortable with his intrusive lens and would often step away so as not be associated with him when he was asked to stop or leave. But she couldn't deny that he often got amazing photos of things others missed.

She peered at the giant platform used for cremation. A man, using a twelve foot stick, tended two fires. One fire had a newly prepared body atop and Maddy wondered if it was the husband of the woman she had seen earlier. The body was draped in a deep orange cloth and bright flames licked at the gold embroidered edge. The attendant worked diligently to stoke the fire, then turned toward the other body which had been burning longer and whose cloth was a powder of ashes. A larger femur bone jutted out of the fire as the keeper worked to roll a blackened skull back onto the ashen heap from whence it had descended. The public cremation was both captivating and horrifying and Maddy again glanced at Richard who had his camera on his knee. Acting like he was blowing out some dust from the tiny dials, he clicked photo after photo.

The boat drifted further downstream near a confluence of other small crafts that held tourists. It was a great spot to photograph the huge gold-domed mosque that rose high above the river. Maddy looked up in awe at the architecture but was quickly distracted back to the water by a buzz that passed from boat to boat. Some people stood up in their small boats rocking them precariously, and gaped out over the water. What looked at first like a large log, rotated and drifted sideways to reveal a human form; a monstrous bloated body was floating down stream. It turned slowly in the current. Richard crouched and shot photos at high speed.

"Oh my God," Maddy said and turned to Naresh. "I thought only ashes were thrown into the river." Her voice pleaded for some reasonable explanation and she tried to figure out how people could bathe and brush their teeth in this water.

Naresh shrugged. "There are some people who are not cremated; Holy men, children, and pregnant women," he said. "Their bodies are blessed and wrapped and weighed down into the water."

"Apparently some pop up." Richard said from behind his camera. The body drifted past and boatmen maneuvered to give it space.

By the time they got off the water and back to the hotel, Maddy was dazed, unable to process all they had seen, heard, and learned that day. She craved a silence that did not exist in this buzzing city. Maddy took off her dirt-encrusted sandals and flicked them into the shower where she sprayed her feet and then collapsed onto the thin bed.

"Don't sleep too long," Richard said. "We are meeting Simon and Rose for dinner tonight."

Maddy groaned and rolled away. "Wake me in an hour."

Her dreams were brief and kinetic, full of moving lights and colors, and left her unrested. She felt compressed when she woke, like the bed had its own gravity from which she struggled to rise. She bathed in a lukewarm shower that was housed in the corner of the room without a curtain. A twelve-inch threshold of blue tiles acted as a barrier and slanted water toward a corner drain. She felt awkward and on display. She scrubbed her face to remove the grime. When she opened a soapy eye, she found Richard watching her. His look was not one of sexual desire but more of curiosity, as though she was both familiar and strange to him. She was thin now after months of trekking, thinner than when they had met years earlier. Maddy perceived her frame as lean, boyish almost, but not youthful and she wondered what he saw. Their relationship was no longer intimate and she turned away from his gaze as a sudden wave of sadness washed over her, onto the slick blue tile, and out into the Ganges.

Simon and Rose were seated at a far corner table of the funky roof top restaurant known for their Bhang Lassi's. The hashish laden yogurt drinks, thick with sweet cardamom, were accompanied by aromatic curries, fragrant jasmine rice and crunchy vegetable Pakora. The Rooftop was a favorite backpacker spot, spread by word of mouth on busses and through hostels. The smell of fresh naan filled the air. Small monkeys skittered about the outer wall and occasionally made a swipe for some food with their thin prehensile hands. Simon waved and stood to hug them in greeting. Rose bubbled over with a tiny squeal and launched into the tale of their twenty hour bus ride from Nepal. Despite her fear of flying, the description of their long bouncy ride made Maddy very happy to have opted for a forty minute flight.

Rose had a thick British accent that contrasted with her jet black hair and almond eyes. Ethnically Chinese, she had been adopted by a British pastor's family and raised in a strict Anglican household in London. After college she ventured out for work and travel and found a job teaching English in Japan where she met Simon. They had worked, saved, and gotten married before launching their world trip. Now in their second year of travel, Simon was eager to get home to Australia. He had backpacked in India years earlier and was less than excited to be back but didn't want to deprive Rose of the experience.

Rose chattered on about the guesthouse and the river while Simon frequently checked a small transistor radio in hopes of catching cricket scores. The Cricket World Cup was just beginning and Simon was easily distracted.

"Where are you planning to go from here?" Rose asked.

"Well, we want to see the Taj Mahal and travel west through Rajasthan," Richard said.

"Oh Simon, we could all travel together." Rose trilled hoping for his excited agreement. Simon nodded blankly, likely in response to the announcer declaring an Arm Ball. Rose clapped and bounced and started planning a course across the top tier of India, Richard throwing in ideas and towns to visit.

Maddy kept one ear in the conversation and one eye on a group of bold monkeys orchestrating a coup. One caramel-colored monkey screeched and leapt onto the dining deck creating a diversion so that his cohorts could swipe food from plates. The waiter, with a full tray in hand, rushed the center monkey and snapped a towel in his direction with a sharp crack. Maddy laughed and thought that the restaurant must be famous for both its hashish yogurt shakes and the monkey entertainment.

Dinner was a feast of curries, Biryani rice, and spicy dahl served up on metal plates in a Thali style meal. Maddy couldn't believe it when the check came and she realized they had eaten like royalty for the equivalent of three American dollars. It would not take long for her to gain back the weight she had shed while trekking. They said goodnight to Rose and Simon and agreed to meet in three days and travel by train to Agra to see the huge fort and the Taj Mahal.

When they got back to the hotel, Richard stayed in the lobby to talk to the owner while Maddy went upstairs. A flash of movement caught her eye when she opened the door. A small monkey darted across the balcony. Before dinner she had washed out her clothes and hung them over the outside chairs to dry. As she approached the balcony, she saw three toddler-sized monkeys and the smaller one who'd swung up onto the wall. Her blue cotton pants were nowhere to be seen and a dark chocolate monkey clutched her tee shirt. The largest monkey gripped her underwear with both hands and bared huge yellow teeth. He delivered a long low hiss as a clear warning. Sensing the confrontation, the little one grabbed a sock and swung quickly out of sight. Maddy had read that monkeys were considered to be incarnations of the goddess Shiva and thus deemed sacred; but to her, they were common criminals. Maybe there was a secret black market of monkey-stolen clothes. She could just see a roomful of trading primates bargaining vigorously over her Adidas socks. The closer she got to the balcony the louder came the warning hiss. Maddy decided that the biggest monkey was tougher than she was, and she did not want to test out her rabies vaccine. Maybe he would donate her clothes to someone needy. Maddy gave one brazen stomp and waved her arms wildly with a loud shout. The troupe let out a squawk, grabbed the remaining laundry and hopped off toward the roof.

She waited several minutes to see if they would return then tip-toed gingerly out on the balcony. Far below, an old man stood in the dim light looking down and up. Holding her bright orange tank top, he searched upward from where it had fallen. Maddy shook her head and decided it was the universe's way of telling her it was time to go shopping.

The remaining days in Varanasi were filled with the paradox that was India; beauty and filth, wealth and poverty, modern and archaic. There was so much to see that Richard and Maddy didn't have to speak much at all, just point to a beautiful shrine or share a strange snack from a street vendor. India was the ultimate diversion. Maddy could only handle the noise and dirt and chaos in small doses. She would eagerly seek out a spice market or tapestry vendor only to become overwhelmed to the point of nausea and retreat to the hotel to sleep and shower and savor the relative quiet of the room.

Electricity went out in cycles and abrasive generators would kick on and churn for hours on end. A festival filled the river at night with tiny floating candles. It looked like a galaxy of stars moving on the sluggish brown current, but this beauty was accompanied by piercing music and loud singing deep into the night. Maddy and Richard were exhausted, but relieved to meet Simon and Rose at the train station, fighting their way onto the third class coach bound for Agra.

The train clicked at the pace of molasses and gave Rose and Richard ample time to talk travel while Simon listened to cricket. Maddy watched the people and countryside beyond the window. For Richard, Rose was a new audience and he told and retold stories that Maddy had heard a hundred times over the course of their marriage; each time the adventure had become more and more fantastic. Maddy shook her head and recalled that his ability to weave a great tale was one of the traits she had initially found interesting about him. But watching him now, he appeared garish, almost comical in his exaggeration to the point of fraud and Maddy found herself more annoyed by the hour.

The trip from Varanasi to Agra took sixteen hours. This was partly due to the infinite stops at every tiny dust-filled village, but mostly, it was because of the cows. Cows had a way of bringing everything in India to a complete halt. As in Nepal, they stood in the streets eating rubbish and diverting traffic into crazy loops and swirls, but today the most problematic cow had taken up residence right on the train track. Just outside of Kanpur, a sable brown cow and her pal, a mangy black and white street dog, parked themselves in the sun on the outbound track. The dog scratched his ears and chewed his paws while the cow licked the dog's back. They were perfectly symbiotic and perfectly unmoving. The train operator, who was inching his way through the outskirts of town, brought the train to a dead stop.

Passengers leaned out the windows to see the cause of the blockade, but their views were obscured by a shanty village that had grown up adjacent to the tracks. A few of the homes were cinderblock and covered in pie sized dung patties placed on the outer walls to dry. The dung would be scrapped off the walls and sold as fuel-patties for cooking fires. Other shelters were made of cloth and cardboard with corrugated metal scraps for roofs. These impoverished dwellings created a narrow chute through which the train would travel and between which the cow and dog were trapped.

A loud honk of the horn sent the dog skittering but word spread through the train that they would just have to wait for the cow to move off the tracks.

"Why doesn't someone just shoo the cow off the tracks?" Maddy asked aloud to no one in particular.

A man across the aisle nodded his head sideways. "There would be nowhere for the cow to go." He said pointing to the tight corridor.

"It just seems ridiculous," Maddy continued, "I'm sure that someone could just lead the cow off the tracks somehow."

"Lead?" asked the man. "The cow is free to go where it

likes."

Maddy furrowed her brows and considered his statement. Cows, in her western paradigm, were herded animals or dinner; she had never considered them as having free will. Simon recognized the look on her face and lowered his radio.

"In the Hindu tradition, cows are considered sacred. That is why they are everywhere. That's where they get the ghee--that oily butter you see on all the shrines. It is used for offerings so the cows are revered and left alone." He raised the radio back to his ear and turned away.

"So we just sit here until the cow decides to move?" Maddy said.

"Oh relax," Richard said. "You are so uptight."

She turned and shot him daggers for his public chastisement but it did not halt his performance, he had a full cabin of people, a captive audience.

"You would think that by now she would be used to traveling, but she still thinks that things should go as planned." Richard laughed a little patronizing laugh and shook his head like a politician.

His barbs stung. Maddy tried to ignore him and turned to the window. The train grumbled to life again and inched forward for ten minutes before finally clearing the shanty tunnel. Children with gritty dark faces lined the tracks and waved as the train picked up speed.

In contrast to the dirty banks of the Ganges, the grounds of the Taj Mahal were a cool green oasis split down the center by a hundred-yard reflecting pool. Indian families were dressed in formal clothes: brilliant saris adorned with gold borders and sparkly jewelry of emerald and gold. People sat alongside the reflecting pool taking photos in hopes of getting that perfect postcard shot of the marble giant in the background.

Rose read aloud the history of the Taj while they stood in line for tickets.

"It was built in 1632 as a mausoleum for Mumtaz Mahal, the third wife of the emperor; she died during the birth of their fourteenth child." Rose looked up from the book to the monolithic marble walls. Archways were ornately carved and inlaid with jewels. White marble towered above and glinted in the sun. They got tickets and entered beneath a lattice of carved marble. The museum offered room after room of masterfully hewn stone carvings and high walls adorned with arching cove windows. Maddy could not imagine the labor that it must have taken to cut such fine patterns into the white stone.

After the tour, they loitered on the thin lawn around the mirror pond and watched the other tourists. Maddy and Richard had maintained their familiar dance; interacting only when necessary, but otherwise they were both happy to use Rose and Simon as emotional buffers. Maddy was still unhappy with Richard's public disrespect of her. I just have to make it through India, she thought. Then what? What would their discussion in Bangkok hold and what did she truly want? Maddy knew that many women travelled alone, but she never envisioned herself able to do it. Maybe it was time for her to pack it in and go home. Richard would have no trouble traipsing around the planet as long as the money held out. Maybe they could find a way to work things out? For now, she just hoped she could survive this filthy, beautiful, amazing, chaotic country. After lounging on the lawn for over an hour, the sun crossed over the Taj. They got up and went in search of dinner.

"I'll do it if you will." Simon said to Richard with a gleam in his eye. They studied a menu of 'Bhang Lassi' and dared each other to order The Black Out.

"Two Black Outs it is." Richard slapped his hand on the table accepting Simon's challenge.

Rose ordered spinach paneer, dahl, and naan for everyone and the waiter returned with two tall glasses, frothy, viscous, and green. Simon took a long slurp and looked up with a hash-yogurt mustache and smiled. "Delicious," he declared.

The mood was light and they talked and laughed about how crazy it was to be away from home for so long. Maddy could tell that Simon yearned to get home, back to the beaches, Australian futbol, and the barbeque.

"You guys will have to come and see us if you come through Melbourne," Simon offered. "We can fire up the barbie and drink some good Aussie beer."

Maddy laughed at his thick accent and agreed that a trip to southern Australia would be fun. She wondered if she and Richard would be together that long. Maddy noticed that the lower the lassi's were in the glass, the louder Richard got. And his stories evolved, even more embellished than usual. His eyelids dropped to half-mast.

"I think we'd better go for a walk." Simon said with a numb tongue, leaning on Rose as he tried to stand. She laughed and guided him toward the door. Richard looked at Maddy. His eyes swam, pupils dilated, and he smiled a stoned lopsided grin. Maddy's stomach turned. This was a familiar scene and one she always disliked. Back home, Richard frequently drank too much and relied on Maddy to take care of him. She resented this role with Richard, and wished for a moment that SHE had ordered the Black Out. She took Richard's heavy arm and helped him stand. He swayed right and left. It was odd to touch him and she shuddered slightly. Maddy steeled herself, supported him about the waist and steered him out into the street.

The roadway was alive with people. Young men hustled by carrying giant flood lights and boxy speakers overhead. Indian pop music blasted through the crowd. It looked like a parade; people of all ages dressed in fine clothing and robust colors moved in rhythm to the pulsing beat. The young men who carried the lights and speakers were tethered together by electrical cords that originated at a clattering gas-powered generator strapped to a cycle rickshaw. Behind the blaring music came a throng of people whistling and pointing and singing toward the center of a moving mob. A young man and woman sat astride decorated horses in a traditional wedding procession. The groom was dressed in a crisp white tunic with gold braiding on the edges. His eyes were dark and lined in charcoal beneath a regal looking turban. Rose peered around to get a look at the bride. The young woman seemed more a girl and was sullen faced but strikingly beautiful beneath a shimmery veil. Her horse was draped in sequined cloth that sparkled when caught by the moving lights.

"The bride does not look very happy." Rose said.

"She looks terrified." Maddy said.

"Let's follow and see where they go." Simon slurred and pushed his way into the crowd. Richard plunged in after him, held up by the sea of bodies. Rose and Maddy ran alongside and were soon swallowed up in the revelers. They flowed down several blocks then veered off into a short alley. The path ended at a large warehouse-like building. White lights twinkled on strings hung around a room filled with long tables. The bride and groom were ushered in and seated with family at the front table.

"Maddy, Maddy." Richard waved his arms wildly. "Over here."

He and Simon were surrounded by adolescent men who laughed and pointed at the tourists who had crashed the wedding party. Oblivious, Richard laughed and tried to high-five them. Totally stoned, he missed their hands, lost his balance and tipped over a chair.

"We need to go." Maddy said, reaching him and righting the chair. "Sorry to intrude."

"Sit. Sit. Eat." Several men said and guided them to a table.

"Yeah Maddy, lighten up and sit down." Richard laughed at his own joke.

She was deeply embarrassed to be an uninvited guest, to be unfamiliar with the customs, and to be sitting next to Richard. The tables filled up quickly and food began to be served. Waiters poured out of the kitchen like locust and swarmed the room with silver pitchers, trays of samosas and giant bowls of curry. They filled plates with steaming food and glasses with chilled water. They cleared dishes and retrieved napkins in a choreographed dance. Silver tongs set a golf ball sized yellow sculpture on Maddy's plate and she studied it in the twinkling light.

"It looks like butter," Rose said and nibbled at the corner of her yellow waxy flower.

"It is a butter samosa," said a nearby man. "It is very expensive. You must try it-very delicious."

"Pure butter?" Maddy asked. A bit on toast was fine, but not to eat in whole globs.

Richard shrugged and popped the butter ball into his mouth.

"Oh crap, that's disgusting," he bellowed and spit the melting ball on the table, yellow liquid oozed from his lips. Guests all around stared at his insolence.

"It is rude to turn back food," said the man who had

150

spoken earlier. "Especially when you are an uninvited guest." Icy stares bored down on all of them.

"I'll go apologize to the bride." Richard said and got up before Maddy could catch him. He stumbled along the row of tables.

"Stop him." Rose barked while she kept a firm hand on Simon who was standing and staring at the twinkling lights.

Richard teetered at the front table and placed his hands flat down around the bride's plate. Her eyes were wide, accentuated by black liner, and she pulled back away from Richard's puffy face. "I just wanted to say thank you for having us and sorry that I spit out the butter golf ball," he slurred. A tiny spray of spittle made the already wide-eyed bride cringe. A bulbous man stepped in front of the table to block Richard from the newlyweds; the man's belt buckle strained under his distended pannus. He grabbed Richard by the shoulders, spun him around, and pushed him toward the door.

"You must go now," the man said.

"Let go of me," Richard yelled and Maddy realized that the entire party was staring at the action by the door. Three crisply dressed men joined in and wrestled Richard to the entrance where he jostled and teetered in feeble attempts to free himself.

"Let's go." Maddy commanded as she caught up with the group, grabbed Richards arm, and yanked him outside. Furious, she shoved him toward the wall where he toppled and sat like a child; legs outstretched, head dangling, fingers greasy with butter. Rose and Simon arrived shortly and laughed at the whole scene.

"I think I'm going to throw up." Richard said.

Maddy shuddered again. "Get up," she said and turned away. "No more lassi's for you - ever," she said.

The next morning, they boarded the train for New Delhi. Simon and Richard laughed at the craziness of the night before and nursed their hangovers. Maddy rode in silence, still angry at Richard for his childish antics and for humiliating them all the previous night. The train got more and more crowded as it inched toward Delhi. Passengers overfilled the third class cabin. Maddy shook her head in disbelief when she saw the front of an oncoming train that had riders pressed to the outside of the car hitching a ride like barnacles on a whale. After hours of cramped travel, the train finally arrived at New Delhi station. Simon had said it was one of the busiest rail stations in the world. Maddy now understood what that meant; getting off the train took the skills of a linebacker.

"When the doors open, put your shoulder down and push," Simon said.

The doors slid back and the heat and reek from the jammed station filled the car. Hordes of passengers began to press onto the train before anyone had disembarked and the chaos rose as people shoved and shouted.

"Follow me!" Simon yelled and made for one of the exits. Maddy, terrified of getting crushed or being left behind, clung to a loose strap on Simon's backpack as he bulldozed his way out. He pushed past a man holding his dark curly-haired daughter, past a Punjabi boy who balanced a bed roll atop his head and past an old hunched woman in a dingy yellow sari with a woven basket on her arm. Adrenalin pumped through Maddy with each step but no matter how hard she pushed, it seemed that the on-flow of people resisted with equal force. The conductor made the initial boarding call for departure and Maddy heard Rose grunting and pushing behind her. Progress was incremental and Maddy was filled with panic and anger.

"This goddam country--why don't they let people just get off first?" She shouted.

At last, Maddy saw the door, took one final breath, and pushed forward with all her might. Still clinging to the tiny strap, she birthed onto the platform. She found her feet on the concrete shuffling among the crowd. Simon was ahead. Rose and Richard were nowhere in sight. Maddy white-knuckled her life-line to Simon. Only twenty steps onto the platform, her feet were halted abruptly by a bag that blocked the entire walkway. Simon must have dodged it somehow, but Maddy was trapped with no way around the people and the suitcases that flanked the bag. She knew that in one second she would tumble over the bag and be crushed beneath thousands of feet. Maddy tried to step over the bag but caught her feet in the handle strap and tripped. She stumbled over the bag spilling its contents onto the concrete like marbles tossed onto a game board. Maddy saw a woman look down in horror as her belongings spewed out onto the platform. Beneath her distressed face, the woman was beautiful with soft caramel skin and shiny black hair. The strap in Maddy's hand went tight then released. Maddy turned away and clawed at the crowd to try to catch Simon again.

She scrambled to her feet and had only taken a few steps when she felt a sharp jerk to her head. It was followed by a bangle-clad fist. With her head pulled skyward, Maddy realized that the women whose bag she had spilled was now holding her hair and punching her face. Maddy twisted to break free and nearly lost her balance stepping on a small tube of lipstick that rolled underfoot. Simon turned back and reached into the frantic fray and grabbed the woman's hand off Maddy's hair. He gave the woman a quick shove. She careened back, arms flailing in her brilliant pink sari as if she were dancing, until she was engulfed by the moving flow of passengers on the platform. Simon grabbed Maddy's pack and hauled her up like a mother cat transporting a kitten. He dragged her out of the station into the open air, bright light, and the craziness of the New Delhi streets.

"What happened in there?" Rose asked when she caught up. A look of concern crossed her face when she noticed the angry glare from Simon who was still holding the scruff of Maddy's pack.

"That woman hit me." Maddy said, "I spilled her bag everywhere."

"Nice job being the ugly American." Richard added

from behind Rose.

"Shut up," Maddy spat, "You're one to talk--wedding crasher."

Maddy could already feel the noise and pollution closing in on her; beggars surrounded them with needy groping hands. "Why don't they let you get off the train before getting on?" she pursued.

Simon looked directly at Maddy. "In India there is no such thing as orderly line, or personal space, or a fixed price, or reliable power; and if that drives you crazy, then it may be time for you to go elsewhere." His words were direct but not condescending, just noting the truths and differences he'd learned from his travels abroad. "It's also very cool--there is no place on earth like it," Simon finished.

Maddy took a deep breath and Rose reached for her hand and said, "Let's go get some lunch. I'm a bit peckish."

Ten

New Delhi was a pulsing mammoth city that resembled an arcade. Vehicles, cows, and lights filled the streets. Men urinated anywhere but there were no women's toilets to be found. Dogs ruled the side streets while monkey's claimed the rooftops. Grime and noise and people and food waste was everywhere. Cars jammed the main streets and wove around the endless pedestrian traffic. The gulf between rich and poor was dramatic; well-groomed portly Brahmins passed by rows of tattered beggars with missing teeth and sunken cheeks. The city was simultaneously enthralling and abominable.

Maddy remained in a foul mood over the next few days in the crush of the huge city. It was not only the overwhelming population that got to her, but Richard seemed worse than ever. Having listened to Rose's lilt for the past week, Richard developed his own British drawl, using new found English terms to berate Maddy: barmpot (clumsy idiot), and bloody cock-up (to have made a mess of things). His jabs at her became more frequent and stabbed sharper than ever. Additionally, the bartering and begging in the streets weighed on her like a leaden blanket.

She longed for a quiet corner, some silent space in which to rest.

Rose talked non-stop and Simon, now back to a full cricket schedule, stayed glued to his tiny transistor radio. At home, Maddy would have gone out for a hike, or taken a walk with Caroline to clear her head. Back home it would have been easy to get some space from Richard.

Over dinner, Maddy stared at Richard while he greedily ate potato samosas and spicy curry drawn up by flesh colored naan. Everything about him had become detestable. She had a sudden urge to leave the table, walk out the door, and be done with it all. She squeezed her eyes shut in an attempt to quiet her mind. In only two days, New Delhi had completely exhausted her. Maddy begged to move on, to a smaller city, to anywhere but there. She made her appeal and the others relented. They agreed to travel west the next morning.

"Hurry!" Maddy yelled as they sprinted toward the curbside motor-rickshaws, "Were going to miss the train!"

They had purchased reserved seats this time, but it was never a guarantee.

"Where would you like to go?" asked the driver in his sing-song tone.

"The train station," Richard replied, "Quickly."

They hefted enormous packs onto the cart and jumped in while Rose and Simon stood negotiating with another driver. Their backpacks were so large now, stuffed with trinkets and tapestries, there was no way the four of them could share a rickshaw. Simon stood in the street patiently bartering the price for a ride to the train station. The tiny motor buzzed to life beneath Maddy and they zoomed off into traffic.

"Do you have the tickets?" Richard asked.

Maddy checked the innermost pocket of her bag and confirmed that she did.

"Oh crap--I have all the tickets," she said. "I have Simon and Rose's tickets too."

Richard pursed his lips and looked back in hopes of seeing them behind, but saw only a sea of motor bikes and rickshaws clogging up the street.

"When we get to the station we're going to have to split up," he said. "I'll leave my bag with you on the train and then run back and find them as they arrive at the station."

"What if the train leaves before you get back?" Maddy asked.

"I don't know--It won't leave," Richard said.

The taxi driver pulled up to the curb abruptly and Maddy handed him some rupees and leapt out. She could barely run under the weight of her pack and she worked hard to follow in Richard's wake. People stared as they blazed a path toward platform number two.

"Where is car ten?" Maddy asked breathlessly to an attendant who motioned them further down the train.

"There." Richard pointed to the car. He jumped on and

dropped his pack into one of the reserved seats. Maddy handed him three tickets like a sprinter handing off a baton.

"What if you can't find them?" she called, but he was already gone.

Maddy offloaded her pack next to Richard's onto one of the four facing seats and tried to fill the whole space to ward off other riders tempted by the open seats. Other passengers boarded and passed by looking at the two giant backpacks they knew she could never have carried there alone. She bit her lip and watched out the window for any sign of Rose or Simon.

A large figure in a bright orange sari appeared at the window; face pressed to the glass in squished distortion. As quickly as it appeared, it was gone. Maddy sat down in an open seat to rest. The conductor began making preparations for departure and made the first boarding call in a deep loud voice. Please hurry, please hurry. At the nearest door, two large women entered the car, one in an orange sari, one in gold. They wore thick dark, poorly applied eyeliner and homicidal red lipstick. Orange Sari was the owner of the contorted face Maddy had seen in the window a moment before and she tried to reconcile the sight of the broad shoulders, smeared make-up, and thick arms. After a few seconds she realized that both Orange Sari and Gold Sari were men.

Gold Sari approached with swaggering hips, grasping at his dress and speaking in Hindi; Orange Sari followed close behind. Maddy stood up to make her presence larger, to claim her seats, and prayed that they would leave her alone.

"No baksheesh--No money," she said signaling no with her hands. Her eyes darted to the window in hopes of seeing Richard or Simon but no one was there. Gold Sari reached with a long soiled finger and stroked Maddy's hair like a serial killer assessing his prize. She swatted his hand away only to notice that he was holding his crotch. Orange Sari raised his hem to expose an ankle, then calf, then a bit of knee.

"Leave me alone." Maddy tried to sound strong but only a whisper escaped her dry lips.

Orange Sari moved in close to her face and breathed hot, sour breath on her neck and Maddy scrambled back in the seat as far as she could. They boxed her in and laughed as Orange Sari slowly raised his skirt above the knee to expose the cleft of his groin.

"Please leave," Maddy tried. "I have nothing you need."

Orange Sari leaned back, supported himself on the bulk of Richards pack, and put his feet up on the seat. Maddy was trapped between his legs. She gulped and tried to scramble back as far as she could, but was jolted upright by the bump of the moving train. Panic swelled as she realized she had no escape from these monsters. Orange Sari licked his lips and sneered in a grotesque display of yellow teeth smeared with scarlet lipstick. With a sick grin, he finally lifted his sari all the way up to expose himself.

He was neither male nor female, but a jumble of both penis and labia. His smile was a bloody smirk. Maddy would later learn that there was a substantial population of hermaphrodites in India that were mostly harmless, if annoying. They made their way by crashing parties and being paid to leave. But at that moment, Maddy could only think of escape. She turned around and tried to bail over the seatback just as Rose came down the aisle, Simon and Richard behind.

"Help!" Maddy yelled halfway over the seatback.

It took only a second for Rose to sum up the situation. "Well!" she huffed in her stiffest British tongue, "That's not nice! That's not nice at-tol!" Her face was severe and scolding and she pointed to the exit like a parochial school principal. Orange Sari dropped the fabric over his legs and the two men left the train.

Maddy, still in shock, slid down into the seat next to Rose. "I thought you guys would never get here," Maddy said.

A moment later, Richard's laugh sliced through the cabin. "That was hysterical. You should have seen your face." He snorted a laugh.

His tone grated in Maddy's head and the sound of rushing water filled her ears. It sloshed in rhythm to her pounding heart. She tried to take a deep breath but found that oxygen wouldn't move; her tongue, thick and pasty, was powder dry.

"Maddy are you ok?" Rose's voice was far away. "Maddy?"

A firm hand gripped her shoulder and Simon gave

Maddy a quick shake.

"Hey--come to," he said.

Maddy's eyes came into focus as the adrenalin-tide receded. The train picked up speed on the outskirts of Delhi. She sat silently. Her backpack on the floor between her legs supported her chin. The pack held the weight of an amazing adventure but was also a cumbersome burden she could barely lift. The grit of India had turned the evergreen canvas to a dingy earth color on the bottom. Small tears along the zippers were beginning to show strain, revealing the lining below. She slept uncomfortably all the way to Jaipur and woke up confused when the train stopped.

Hours away from New Delhi, the sky was clear. It was evident upon exiting the train station, that Jaipur was different. Vendors and taxis were present but not overwhelming. The sidewalks were not overrun with beggars or cows, and no one yelled or collided in the street. Maddy smiled and realized that for the first time in weeks, she could hear herself think.

On the ride to the Jaipur Inn, Rose marveled at how wide the streets were, and how they intersected at orderly intervals. The travel guide referred to Jaipur as the 'Paris of India;' a cultural center of Rajasthan often noted for its amazing architecture. Highlights included the Palace of the Wind and the Amber Fort. Maddy rode in silence and enjoyed the clean air and beautifully dressed women who walked along the road carrying shopping bags and totes of vegetables; silver ringed toes peeked out modestly from under colorful sari fabrics. The hotel entrance was through a quaint garden with small tables tucked under arbors and blooming trellises. Maddy breathed in the deep fragrance of jasmine and lavender.

Because of a few days break in the cricket schedule, Simon took on the role of tour guide and planned out several days of sight-seeing. Rose bubbled and chattered and pointed at interesting buildings and complex tapestries. Richard continued his grandiloquence. Maddy was quiet. She wanted to enjoy the peace of this city, the hotel garden and the clear air without the pollution of their relationship. She went along for the ride, watched and listened, but kept to herself. On the last afternoon in Jaipur, the quartet set out to see the giant Amber Fort that towered above the city. It was built in 1592 as a palace. The fort, made of red sandstone and marble, was constructed around the royal dwelling. It stood like a high-rise against the hillside and reached toward the sky.

Maddy stood at the base of the fort, mouth agape, staring at the long winding walkway that climbed and curved up to the fort entrance. Elephants draped in embroidered tapestries lumbered up and down the expansive path offering transport to the entrance. Their giant, whisper-soft feet moved in a fluid rhythm despite the tremendous mass they carried. Mesmerized, Maddy signaled to the mahout. He pointed her toward a platform next to the path and she skittered there. Before she could climb the stairs, a small hand closed around her fingers.

Maddy looked down to find a young boy, a beautiful brown eyed-boy, gently holding her hand. A wondrous grin broke across her face and the mahout laughed out loud.

"This is my son, Vasur." The man beamed with pride.

"I will take her to the main gate, Babu." The boy's voice was high and soft. The mahout nodded making the boy smile. Maddy melted at the small tug of his soft fingers and she followed the boy up the long winding ramp. She heard Richard's voice, distant and inconsequential, as she and Vasur rounded the first curve. They passed carved sandstone walls and patterned mosaics that represented the art and history of the fort. Snake charmers lined the path with baskets of cobras who danced to minor key notes emanating from gourd-shaped flutes.

Maddy looked down at the creamy sun-kissed skin of the boy and asked, "What is your favorite place at the fort?"

"Ohhh, I love the Ganesh Gate," Vasur said without hesitation.

"Who is Ganesh?" Maddy asked.

"He is the God of new beginnings. He will take away all your troubles." The boy spoke like an old Hindu scholar, a reincarnation of a wise spiritual man.

Maddy's breath caught in her chest. Suddenly, she had to see the Ganesh Gate.

"Hurry," the boy said. "We must see Ganesh before the sun is down."

She did not know why her feet took up the urgency

of his words, but she darted past the elephants and wove between pedestrians as the light began to angle shadows through the carved cut outs. They crested the last incline and crossed under the massive stone entrance of the Sun Gate. It was once used for victory parades of armies returning from battle and it opened onto Jaleb Chowk, a huge courtyard and assembly area. Maddy could imagine the battle weary fighters being met by worried and proud family members after days of protecting the fort. People stood in groups all around; some followed tour guides who spoke and gestured with great animation while other tourists just wandered about the courtyard.

Vasur tugged her hand and led her down cavernous hallways and alcoves dotting the edge of the courtyard. Across the expanse, people were ascending a long marble staircase. They sprinted toward the stairs and Vasur giggled when Maddy jumped up the first few taking two at a time. Breathless at the top of the staircase, she caught a glint of metal that pulled her attention toward an ornate multi-paneled door. It was titled The Silver Door and no longer opened, but sat on display to showcase the God Shiva. Pictures of Shiva in different incarnations had been meticulously framed in silver and were inset in the panel from top to bottom; Shiva on a Brahma bull or sitting within a lotus flower, multiple arms held out in address. The light slid gently over the polished relief.

"This way," Vasur said.

Adjacent to the silver door was a hallway that led to the

old quarters of the private palace. Maddy and the boy ran down the hall hand in hand and stopped at the end. There, in the soft light of the late afternoon sat a full size statue of Lord Ganesh. Above the arched doorway the sign read: The Ganesh Gate. The statue of Ganesh was made of pink coral and absorbed the light from nearby windows. It glowed with a rose-petal hue as if a candle burned within. Its being was curious, part elephant, part human with a short trunk and four arms. Each arm held a symbolic item: a piece of broken tusk, a bowl of sweet delicacies, a rope and an axe. She had no idea what these icons symbolized, but she was drawn to the energy of the figure. *'Lord of New Beginnings, Remover of Obstacles,'* she read on the placard next to the statue. She placed both hands on the cool coral and closed her eyes. Help me find my way, her lips whispered. Please make my path clear. When she opened her eyes the light within the statue flared bright for one moment, then turned cool as evening fell into the hall.

Maddy turned to look for Vasur, to hug him, to thank him, but he was gone. Instead, she saw Richard coming toward her.

"There you are." Richard's voice shattered the space. "Why did you take off? What the hell is wrong with you?"

Maddy looked at him. Her eyes fixed on his craggy face, her feet already moving away from him. Richard came toward her but she stepped through the Ganesh Gate and broke into a run. She ran through the high ceilinged Palace of Mirrors, where her hundred-fold reflection fled by; she ran past the magic-flower fresco of carefree butterflies that danced around the emerging petals of a new bud. She followed no path, taking hallways and turns as each presented itself until she emerged into a cool courtyard beneath a sandalwood door labeled the Hall of Pleasures. The light was amber with dusk. A channel of water bisected the plaza and the sound of her feet bounced off the high walls. A staircase led her up and up to the crest of the outer wall. She stood high above the city and lost her breath at the view of the houses below. Shadows of blue and white roofs dotted the landscape with doors painted in deep reds, yellows, and greens. She scanned the fort to find the long elephant walkway. Breathless again, in a flat run, she hurtled down the curving incline, gaining speed as she flew. She ran with abandon, giddy with release as she spilled out into the wide streets of Jaipur.

Eleven

Her hands shook as she laid the note on the bed. What was there to say? She was afraid that if she paused to think, she would change her mind. The note was simple:

> *Dear Richard -*
> *I could not stay any longer. I hope you find*
> *happiness.*
> *Goodbye.*
> *Maddy*

She split the stack of traveler's checks and laid a small pile on the note. At the door she paused, dug into her passport pouch and felt for her wedding ring. Its smooth edges contrasted with the craggy points of her marriage. She turned it over in her hand one last time and then laid it on the note and left.

The evening traffic was rising as she walked a block to catch a rickshaw.

"Where are you going madam?" asked the driver.

Panic hit her like a cricket bat and she stared at him with

wide, frozen eyes.

"Madame?" He called out to her; his musical voice was distant and played at thirty-three speed. She pushed herself toward it until he came into focus.

"The train station," she whispered.

Oh shit. What had she done? Where was she going? She wandered to the ticket window and purchased a ticket to Calcutta. The ticket person furrowed her brow and asked, "Are you sure you want the first train out? It's very slow."

The first train out was in fact, the mail train. It stopped every hour at dusty platforms in the middle of nowhere. In the morning, Maddy woke early to fog and the call of tea sellers chanting out 'chai-chai.' A dark hand pushed a tiny clay cup of tea through the window slot and she exchanged it for a few rupees. She bought hard boiled eggs and curried potatoes steamed in banana leaves from a hunched woman pushing a creaky cart through the cabin. Maddy stared out the window at children who ran almost the speed of the crawling train. She felt disjointed, unable to fully comprehend the impact of her impulsive decision.

Forty-three hours later, Maddy stepped off the train onto the crowded platform. Calcutta was yet another Indian paradox. Neon lights blinked off the faces of haggard beggars. People jostled bedrolls and parcels, children and baskets. The smell of sweat mixed with cloves from bubbling pots of chai. She looked around trying to get her bearings. Previously she had relied on Richard to lead the way. But now, she cinched up her pack and followed the flow of the crowd.

The station was filled with people from all walks of life; wealthy well dressed women wearing rhinestone-pocket jeans waited beside women in pale, battered saris. The chatter of Hindi and English created a busy hum in the warm air. Maddy walked by rows of scraggly children holding dented copper bowls in outstretched arms. She veered out of the crowd and dug into her pocket for some rupee coins. As Maddy bent to drop the coins in the dusty bowl, slender fingers encircled her wrist. A thin woman in a faded pink sari stood close to her. In her arms was the limp body of a young boy. The woman stared directly into Maddy's face.

"My son is sick. Will you help us to a hospital?" She asked.

Maddy looked around for an easy escape but felt the desperation in the woman's grasp. The child stirred slightly and opened his eyes. The boy had the slow-eyed blink of exhaustion. His deep brown eyes looked far away.

"I am Diya. This is Aarush. Please help us to the hospital," she pleaded.

Maddy looked around at the people passing by. No one stopped or even noticed them standing in the walkway. No one paid any mind to the sick boy. Maddy recalled being ill in Egypt and how a Jack and Amina had washed her, dressed her, and carried her across the sand to the doctor. She had been so thankful of his selfless act.

"Of course," Maddy said to Diya. "Let's go."

They bumped through travelers, swimming upstream until they made it out to the street. Rickshaws and cabs lined the road eager for a fare. Maddy waved a hand and four drivers rushed forward.

"Very good price for you," one driver called.

"Madam, I have a good hotel for you," another shouted.

Maddy shook her head. "We need a hospital."

"Which hospital?" The tuk-tuk driver glanced at the boy and helped Diya into the cart.

"Mother Teresa hospital." Diya said. The driver nodded and weaved into traffic.

A charity hospital was bound to be spare but Maddy was taken aback when they were dropped beneath a plaque that read: Home for the Sick and Dying Destitute. The volunteer at the paltry desk pointed them towards the women's respite area. The hospital was less of a care center and more of a dormitory. Rows and rows of narrow beds were covered in thin bedroll pads. Having worked for a hospital back home, Maddy had seen the two-patient rooms converted to single occupancy with each remodel project. For Americans, being sick was a private affair. Not so here. Women lay on cots in varying degrees of lifelessness. Many coughed while others moaned, creating a sorrowful symphony. A volunteer lifted a child from the arms of a woman so thin it was impossible she was still alive. Diya looked about and saw an empty bed. Maddy followed and they took Aarush and laid him down. He was limp, past crying. He didn't stir.

"Please -- a nurse," Diya said.

Maddy nodded and looked down the cavernous room of cots. She tiptoed past women with mouths agape and children whose breath rattled deep and raspy. She tried not to look, terrified that she might be mistaken for a volunteer. Maddy's life had not been one of service. She had never volunteered, never thought about helping others. She had worked for hospitals but only on the sterile business end of things. Even when applying for university, she had used her work as a YMCA camp registrar as meeting her 'community engagement' requirement. Her life had been sheltered from the hardships of others. She had never seen anyone die, not even her own baby. Her heart pounded at the idea that she might fail, that she would not find a nurse in time, or despite her effort, that Aarush would die.

Beyond the women's dorm was a corridor. Additional rooms opened to the left and to the right of the hallway. A smell like no other, funky and rank, assaulted her nostrils as she entered the first men's dormitory. Three men, a Hindu priest and two volunteers, were busy wrapping the body of a newly deceased man. They used the sheet to swaddle the thin frame such that the sheet formed both a covering and a sling. Swinging slightly the body was lifted from the cot. A mixture of red and brown liquid leaked from the low dip in the sheet and dripped a line of oozing fluid across the floor as the volunteers moved the body to wheelbarrow style cart. Another man came up behind with a mop and bucket to swab the floor. The priest pressed his hands over his lips whispering prayers above the dead man's body.

Tightness caught in Maddy's throat. Her previously intimate concept of death was filleted open. Though the body was handled with adequate respect, she was struck by profound sadness at the scene. Farther down the room, a squat Latino volunteer lifted a man from his bed and carried him toward the shower area. The patient's extremities bounced limply with each step, knees and elbows jutting outward. Near to the door sat two men on a cot sharing stories in Urdu. Neither one had teeth. Maddy scanned the room and waved to a volunteer and asked about a nurse. The volunteer shrugged, his arms occupied by a rusted bedside commode. He nodded toward the hall.

The next room looked like an old fashioned locker room with toilets on one wall facing showers on the opposite side. Several men sat on the commodes; one drooped forward as if asleep over his lap, another with his head propped in his hands. All privacy was gone. Maddy was embarrassed by their exposure. Standing at a sink, she saw a man rise from washing his hair. The dripping grey strands reached down past his waist. With care, he wrung out the water and then entwined the hair into a length of white fabric. Then, in a complex swirl and twist, the hair was mounted into a turban atop his head. He nudged it gently to center balance.

At the end of the hallway Maddy could hear the chatter of children. This ward was as large as the previous ones but slightly more animated. Some of the children lay quietly on cots, but others congregated in a circle and tossed a worn red ball between them. A white scarfed nun bobbed into view. She wore a floor length robe, only her face and hands were uncovered. Blue stripes bordered the scarf and framed her lined cheeks.

"Hello," Maddy said. "Can you help my friend? Her son is very ill." Maddy motioned down the hall. The sister did not reply, but tucked her box of medications up on a high shelf and followed.

Maddy held her breath as they approached. Diya lay curled around the still body of Aarush. Diya sat up and spoke to the sister in Hindi. The nun replied in Spanish. Maddy surmised that this hospital was staffed only by religious people and volunteers from around the world. It seemed there were no real medical people to be found. The sister touched Aarush's forehead, looked at his gums, and pinched the turgor of his skin. It was not unlike a veterinary assessment. Even if she had no formal medical training, it was comforting to have someone attend to the boy. The nun touched Diya's shoulder and then left. Diya looked to Maddy with pleading eyes, but Maddy had no advice to offer. She sat on the bed and stroked the boy's hair.

An eternity passed. Diya fell asleep next to Aarush. Not knowing what else to do, Maddy sat on the edge of the bed. A different nun, one who spoke a little English appeared and handed Maddy a narrow syringe filled with a liquid the color of malt-o-meal.

"Feed the boy," the nun instructed. "Find a way to wake him enough to eat."

174

Maddy stared at the syringe. "How?" But the nun had already left. Maddy stared at Aarush. He was probably older than he looked, but due to his state, he seemed barely a toddler. His tiny frame was lifeless on the flimsy cot. Maddy approached and gently shook the boy. His body jiggled softly but he did not stir. She went to lift him but realized she did not know how. She knew nothing about caring for a child. She had never even done any babysitting, instead she had cleaned houses in high school and college. She was afraid to pick up the boy, lest she drop him, so she sat on the cot and awkwardly maneuvered Aarush into her lap. He was light and limp as a rag doll. Diya snored softly next to her.

"Aarush," Maddy said. "Wake up. Time to eat." She jostled him as she spoke. His eyes remained heavy. She picked up a leg and shook it. When there was no response, she gave his foot a squeeze. Aarush withdrew his foot. Knowing she had to get him awake, she caught him under the armpits and lifted him upright bouncing his body. "Wake up, wake up," she repeated. Dark brown eyes peeked out from under his leaden lashes. She quickly returned him to her lap and slid the syringe into his mouth.

"Please drink little one," Maddy whispered, pleading silently for him to stay awake. The gruel filed his mouth by the ounce and he swallowed reflexively. Liquid dribbled from the corners of his mouth and Maddy wiped it away. Little by little the syringe was emptied. She tucked Aarush under his mother's arm to sleep.

She left the dimness of the hospital to find a hotel. The brightness of daylight disoriented her. In the past few days she had gone from sight-seeing with Richard, Rose, and Simon, to leaving her husband and landing in an Indian hospital feeding a dying child. She was suddenly exhausted, unmoored, and dirty from the two day train ride. Deep fried Samosas reminded her that she was also hungry. Unwilling to haggle, she happily overpaid the vendor and left with a handful of savory vegetable dumplings.

Maddy walked several blocks and found a postage stamp sized room at the Hotel Diplomat, a dingy backpacker joint where the owner apologized for not having electricity at the moment but promised it would 'be back soon.' Street noise penetrated the walls and she lay face up on the bed watching the motionless fan blades for signs of life. She tried the faucet but no water came. At the front desk, she pleaded for some water to wash off two days of travel grit. She was told that it would be delivered to her room, soon.

Two hours later, a loud knock woke her up. A man stood there, holding the strangest implement she had ever seen. It was a giant bladder or an animal hide of sorts, carried like a bagpipe and filled with water. The man hoisted the bladder up, placed a bucket down, and with a forceful squeeze, he expelled water from the carcass-vessel. She gawked in amazement and then smiled at the ingenuity. Maddy tipped the water-piper and he left. Squatting inside the bucket amounted to an awkward birdbath that was more struggle than grace and it reminded her of Caroline's description of farmyard chickens in the wading pool on a hot day. Maddy sighed. She knew it was time to call her mother.

"You did what?" Caroline asked in a high frequency voice.

"I left Richard."

"Left-left? Or just taking a breather?"

"Left-left. I left a note and got on a train."

"Oh my, he must have had a fit." Caroline said and pictured an apoplectic Richard holding the scribbled message.

"Where are you now?"

"I'm in Calcutta. I think I may be here a while," Maddy said.

Silence occupied the line. Finally Caroline came back. "Why are you staying there? Do you like it? Is it nice?"

"I haven't really seen much of the city. I got side tracked coming off the train." Maddy explained what had happened.

Again, there was no reply but this time not from the bad connection.

"That is terrible," Caroline said. "Do the doctors think the boy will survive?"

"I don't think there are any doctors at this hospital. It's more like a place the poor people go when they are dying, then it's up to fate from there." Maddy replied. Without warning, Maddy burst into tears. She had cried so many times over the past months because of her fear of flying and from dealing with Richard, but this was different. Her relationship woes with Richard seemed foolish, embarrassing now in light of real hardship, faced with the reality of a dying boy. A guttural anguish plunged through her and she crumpled down into the corner beside the front desk counter. Her breath squeezed out forever, as if breathing in would never be possible again. She must have scared the hotel clerk for he followed the phone cord and leaned over the counter with an uncomfortable look on his face.

"Mom, I'm scared," Maddy wheezed when she could finally draw a breath. The line was empty. No reassuring voice comforted her. No soothing words were delivered. No wisdom from her mother. Maddy stared at the dead line for a full minute. She considered calling her mother back, but knew she only had a minute or two left on the international calling card.

Back in her room, Maddy took stock. She needed to figure out what to do. She couldn't let Aarush die. If she offered to take him to a real hospital and pay the bill, it would deplete all her money. Then again, she may soon have no money at all if Richard was angry enough to close their shared bank account. And what if Aarush recovered? Where would he and Diya go? Where would Maddy go? She knew she only had enough travel money for a few months. She would have to be very frugal. Then there was the reality that at some point she would have to go home and deal with her house, with Richard, and their shared belongings. The idea of this added weight to her already heavy heart. But first, she needed to check on Aarush. Maddy washed her face and stopped by a food cart on the way to Mother Teresa Hospital. She picked up hot buttered naan and chai tea hoping a little food would help them all.

Diya's eyes lit up when she saw Maddy in the doorway. Diya's teeth were crisscrossed in front and Maddy noted that this was the first time she had seen the woman smile. She had a mole at her temple that moved when she smiled. Her face brightened further when Maddy offered the naan. Diya tore at the buttery bread, savoring each bite.

"When did you last eat?" Maddy asked, acutely aware that eating was a luxury she had always taken for granted. Diya lowered her eyes and bobbled her head. "A while ago," she replied.

Aarush stirred and opened sleepy eyes. He looked toward his mother and motioned to his mouth.

"Water," Diya said. Maddy poured water into the cap of her bottle and gave him sips by the thimble. When he closed his eyes, Maddy offered the bottle to Diya who finished it off and accepted tea as well.

"He seems better," Maddy said, relief flooding her body. "Maybe a few more days of food and he will be up and moving."

Diya nodded, her mouth full of bread.

"Where will you go when he is better?" Maddy asked. "Are you from Calcutta?"

Diya shook her head. "I am from Kumar Khali, Bangladesh, near the Gorai River." She spoke quickly as a child eager to talk but then dropped her head. "But I cannot go home."

"Why? Do you have any family there?"

Diya nodded. "My mother is passed but my father and sisters are there." She stopped again. A furrow in her brow deepened and she squeezed her hands in a tight clasp. "My father sent me away when he learned of the baby. He paid a very bad man to take me to a home for girls. But I did not go there." Diya stopped chewing as though the bread had turned to clay in her mouth. Maddy realized just how young this mother was.

"What happened?" Maddy asked.

"I ran away in the night, holding my belly to run as fast as I could. I slept in the brush away from the road to hide from the bad man. Finally, Aarush came." Diya's closed eyes moved behind the lids as though a movie were being re-run inside there. "His name means sunshine." Diya smiled faintly.

"He is beautiful. Surely your father would like to see his grandson, no?"

Diya shook her head. "I cannot go home with a child. I have no husband. I have shamed my family."

"There has to be a way to convince him, to show him that your boy is part of the family," Maddy said.

"You would not understand. Your country is different. My father is very traditional. He has a small business exporting rice. It would be very bad for his business to have a shameful daughter and grandson live in his home." Diya shook her head. She gathered her sari around her and lay down next to Aarush.

Maddy wandered the streets of Calcutta in the evening. She wondered what it would be like to have so few options, not to mention being rejected by her family. She knew she was very fortunate to have an education and tangible work skills. Even in this time of transition in her own life she knew she could go home any time, get a job, and be able to support herself.

The crack of a cricket bat turned her head. Maddy had walked away from the busy market area and was near the Colonial Museum. A cricket match was being played on the sparse lawn. Men and boys were dressed in crisp white shirts and trousers. The pitcher sailed a ball at the batter who smacked it high overhead. One team cheered as the players advanced the score. It looked like a confusing baseball game and Maddy marveled at how clean the men's uniforms were despite the heat and dust. Just another paradox of India.

That night, the bed felt huge and empty and the power went out in cycles. The continual street noise distracted Maddy from the reality that she was alone and didn't know what to do next. She tried not to dwell on the radical changes that her life had taken in the past week. It felt like being with Richard was already a lifetime ago. In the morning she picked up more naan, some boiled eggs and spicy chutney, and headed to Mother Teresa hospital. She greeted the front entry volunteer and went into the women's dorm.

The cot where Diya and Aarush had slept yesterday was empty. Maddy scanned the room to see where they had moved. An old woman with wrinkles like spider webs across her face motioned for Maddy to come over.

"Do you know where the woman and boy moved to?" Maddy asked.

The elder patted her bedroll for Maddy to sit down. "She left in the night," the woman said. Her tongue moved among bare gums. "They moved the boy to the children's area."

"Moved him? She left?" Maddy tried to comprehend. "No, she couldn't have left. Why would she leave Aarush here?" She stared toward the empty cot trying to make sense of this news.

The woman patted Maddy's hand to imply her youth and naivety. "Many women leave their children here. They know that they will be fed. That is why the sisters run the orphanage."

"No, No. This can't be," Maddy said. "He was sick. She would have at least stayed until he was well."

"The boy was up and walking early this morning. He looked stronger." The elder's eyes were milky white and Maddy wanted to believe that the old woman was too blind to know what had happened. But the cot was empty. Maddy sat with her mouth agape for several minutes. The woman pointed to the bag of food that Maddy held. Maddy untwirled the plastic from her wrist and handed it to her.

"Where is the boy?" Maddy asked again.

Already with a mouthful of naan, the woman pointed down the hall.

The sound of children's voices puckered the air in the dormitory at the end of the hall. Maddy took in the mass of children who filled the room. She searched each face for Aarush. His dingy red shirt grabbed her attention. He sat opposite another boy. They shared a plate of rice, scooping it up with their fingers into hungry mouths. Maddy went toward the boy but was intercepted by a nun who stepped into the path between the cots. Her habit was askew on her damp face.

"Are you looking for someone?" She spoke clear English with only a fleck of Italian.

"That boy." Maddy pointed. "I was here with his mother. But today she is gone."

The sister nodded. Waited for more. When Maddy did not to go on she said, "He will stay here now."

"But, but, will she come back for him? Why did she leave?"

"Sometimes we never know." The sister crossed herself and raised her eyes toward heaven. Maddy's mouth opened and closed without words. She wanted to go over to Aarush, to speak to him and tell him... tell him what? That everything would be ok?

"If you want to help him you can make a donation."

The nun pulled a damp envelope from her apron. Maddy looked back to Aarush. His beautiful face held a smile as he and the other boy made silly motions with their hands. She waved but he continued to play. A hollow feeling surrounded her heart and she turned away. She stuffed the communion sized envelope with all the US dollars she had on her and dropped it into the box at the exit. Mindlessly, she dipped her finger tips into the chalice of holy water hoping for relief, but her fingers hit the copper bottom. The bowl was empty.

Twelve

Traffic moved like honey from the Bangkok airport along Ratchawithi Road. The sticky, humid bus dropped Maddy on Kho San Road. The backpacker's ghetto, known for its tee-shirt hawkers and cheap rooms, gave Maddy a small feeling of comfort since she and Richard had stayed there before Nepal. She took a room at Ranee Guest House and dropped herself and her pack on the bed. Thankfully, a breeze wafted down from the ceiling fan. She thought about getting up, but did not move. The humidity glued her to the bed. She felt leaden and confused. Maddy was exhausted from flying even though it had been uneventful. Her whole world was in limbo now. She had thought that she might have felt happy, euphoric even after leaving Richard, but she was only tired. She was still in shock over Diya leaving Aarush in the children's ward in Calcutta. Nothing made sense.

An hour later, she dragged herself to the shower. The cool water soothed her tight muscles and she began to feel better. Until she saw the spider. An involuntary shriek left her lips and she backed up against the flowing facet. On the wall just above the stall door, perched a plate-sized spider.

Hairy legs clutched the edges of a sign that read, "Turn Water Off Fully."

Maddy did as directed and shivered despite the warm air. How was she going to get out? The only weapons she had were a pair of two-dollar flip flops and a micro-sized bottle of shampoo. It became clear that her only real option was to flee, to sprint underneath the looming arachnid. She wanted to yell for help, but who would come? And what would they do? Good thing Richard was not here, she thought, he would have laughed hysterically.

Gingerly, Maddy plucked her towel from the hook and gave herself a pep talk. "It's time to buck up" she mumbled. Before she could finish her monologue, the spider moved. Maddy screamed, threw her towel over her head and flung open the door. She bolted buck naked from the shower stall in a full shrieking battle-cry. Her wet, blind trajectory was halted abruptly when she ran head long into Neils, the guesthouse owner's husband. Neils spun, trying to keep ahold of the boxes he carried. She maneuvered the towel to her torso and made it back to her room.

Embarrassed, but clean and dressed, Maddy towel dried her hair. She remembered the romantic ideas she had had about traveling. She had envisioned herself sitting next to a tranquil lake sipping handmade lemonade in the sun. She had never imagined herself running naked from a spider the size of her hand. Then again, she never envisioned herself in Bangkok alone. She resisted the urge to lie down and forced herself to find some dinner.

186

Neon lights buzzed along Kho San Road luring backpackers in for food, videos, and travel arrangements. Maddy remembered that travel agents had magic ways of getting tickets and Visas in just days when it usually took weeks to obtain through a consulate. Bangkok was the ultimate hub. It was possible to fly, train, or bus out to anywhere in the world. She sat at a wobbly table and ate Pad Thai while looking at her journal. She needed to figure out what to do. It seemed a shame to go home now knowing that she might never be back on this side of the world again. Besides, nothing awaited her back home. Just enough money remained for a few more months if she was frugal. She stared at the agents' listing board of flights. Where to go? Singapore, Kuala Lumpur, Phnom Penn, Saigon, Bali, Rome? She needed some travel guides to explore before making a decision. Tomorrow she would find a book store.

In the morning she got directions to a small shop called Ethan's Books. Maddy turned down a crooked alley and the door chime tinkled when she walked in. Wall to wall books made her feel at home. She stood in front of the travel books and scanned the shelves.

"If you were going to die in one month what would you see before it happened?" Ethan, the Australian-accented owner, stood behind Maddy surveying the plethora of travel guides.

Maddy shook her head, "That's quite a question. There are just so many places to go. Do you have any recommendations?"

He rubbed the blond stubble on his chin. "If you like water I suggest Bali or Australia; for ancient ruins you can't miss Cambodia; Vietnam is cheap and brimming with tourists."

Still confused and not used to making decisions on her own, she stared at the guide books with their sharp white titles. "Um, I don't really love the water, so I'll take ruins for two-hundred."

Ethan laughed, reached up and pulled out the Lonely Plant guide for Cambodia. He thumbed through the pages until he found a picture of Angkor Wat, a giant Hindu temple outside the town of Siem Reap.

"It's truly spectacular," he said.

She recalled that Cambodia was a place Richard had marked with a red star on the map at home, but it had seemed so distant then that she had not done any research.

"What's the best way to get there?" She said.

"By air, that's how I went," he said.

"When were you there?" Maddy asked

"Two years ago just before I opened up this place."

"How did you end up here?" Maddy asked.

"Ah, now that's a long story. The short version is I followed my girlfriend here. Unfortunately, things didn't sort out for us, but I loved Bangkok and stayed."

Maddy nodded knowingly and turned back to the stacks. "Have you been to Vietnam?" she asked.

"Aw, yeah," he said. "It's booming with development. The Mekong River trip is great and Halong Bay is brilliant; limestone pillars jutting out of the water."

"It sounds interesting." She paged through the Vietnam guidebook. It had also been starred on her map at home although she didn't recall why or who had recommended it.

"Are you traveling alone?" Ethan asked.

It was a question she would have to get used to. "Yeah, well that too is a long story," she sighed. "I started out with my husband but we split up a few weeks ago."

"Ouch. That's pretty recent. How are you holding up?" he asked. Ethan's accent had a way of making him sound casual while asking an intimate question.

"I'm mostly numb," she said. "This is actually the first time I've told anyone this face to face. Crazy-huh?"

"Traveling is like that though. You can almost get more comfortable with total strangers. Known people are too much of an investment." He smiled a crooked smile.

Maddy understood this strange sentiment. She recalled the procession of transient acquaintances she had met on her journey. Some she had known for only a few hours or days but found herself telling them more about her life than most of her friends back home.

"Is it safe to travel alone to Vietnam and Cambodia?" Maddy returned to her task.

"As safe as any place," he said, "as long as you use your head. Don't take any drugs and look like you know what you're doing--project confidence."

189

She would have to work on that since she truly felt like she hadn't a clue.

"Ok then, I'll take both these books," she said.

"Be sure not to miss the temples here in Bangkok," he recommended.

Without any better ideas, she decided to follow his suggestion. Maddy started by finding the Temple of Wat Pho. It was a traditional Thai temple painted with gold and red trim on the pagoda-style roofs. Wat Pho was named after a monastery in India where the Buddha lived as a young man. The temple was famous because it housed the one-hundred-forty-one foot golden Reclining Buddha. The giant gold Buddha, stretched on its side, filled an entire room. The serene genderless face was transcendent and the smooth gold shone all the way down to the soles of its feet which were inlaid with one hundred and eight panels of mother of pearl. Each panel held a symbol that represented the Buddha is some form: lotus flower, dancer, an elephant. Each engraved figure was detailed with shimmery edges that changed color in the light. Maddy sat still before the statue, captivated by the serenity it embodied and thankful for the opportunity to pause and slow her mind.

This was the first time she had been without Richard since she was twenty-one. No wonder it felt so strange. Her main hope for years was to be part of a 'we,' to achieve the elusive marital bliss. In marrying Richard just out of college, she had gained a partner in the combining sense but never found the deep connection she was hoping for.

Looking back now, it seemed ridiculous that she had wanted it or thought that it was possible with him. She felt as if she had spent years walking in circles looking for an entry point into their relationship when none existed; the barriers they had both erected were impenetrable.

She lingered in the Buddha's presence hoping to absorb its equanimity. Its silent contemplation reminded her of the note she had tucked into her journal several months back--look for writing by Rumi. She recalled Galiana's blissful smile that accompanied the reading recommendation. Maddy slipped from the reclining Buddha, added a coin to one of the one-hundred and eight copper bowls outside the temple and headed back to the backpackers' ghetto. She passed her guesthouse and continued on to Ethan's Books.

"You're back," Ethan said with a warm smile when she came through the door.

"I forgot to look for a book on my list," she said. "Do you have anything by Rumi?"

His grin widened and he went several stacks back. "Searching for more than tourist sites then?"

"Aren't we all?" she said.

He handed her two small books, the covers crinkled with use. One was a collection of short quotes, the other of poems. She paged open the small quotation book and read the first passage that leapt forward:

Let yourself be silently drawn by the stronger pull of what you really love.

She absorbed the meaning of the words and stood still next to Ethan.

"Read more, out loud," he requested. "His words are most beautiful when spoken."

He leaned in toward the book and Maddy read:

You have been walking the ocean's edge, holding up your robes to keep them dry. You must dive deeper under, a thousand times deeper.

Her eyes filled before she could even register the words. She blinked quickly to clear her vision.

Ethan pointed to a phrase, "Read that one."

Maddy cleared her voice and spoke softly:

Forget safety, live where you fear to live. Destroy your reputation. Be notorious.

She smiled and held the book to her chest, transfixed by the invitation to let go, to forget safety. Ethan waited in silence as she let the words wash over her, the lines on her face forming and releasing tiny creases.

"I don't know how," she said. "Never have."

He patted her shoulder. "Start small. Write the passage every morning in your journal then decide what to do. Always look for people who have a story that teaches you something about life. It's the most brilliant thing about traveling, learning about yourself through the people you meet.

"Great advice," she said. "I'll do my best." She paid and turned to the door.

"Don't forget to come back and tell me about your notoriety," he laughed and waved goodbye.

Thirteen

The plane descended in a tight spiral toward Phnom Penh and Maddy squeezed her eyes shut and clutched the armrests.

"Why are we landing on a turn?" she cried out involuntarily as the plane held a tight left bank, its wing pointing toward the ground. At the last second, the plane leveled just before the wheels touched down in the capital of Cambodia.

Maddy emerged from customs onto the street. She was blasted by the buzz of motor bikes that filled lanes in both directions. Young men with black hair and sunglasses waved at travelers and motioned to the rear of their bikes.

Skeptically she approached one and asked, "No moto-taxi? No bus?"

The young man shook his head and pointed to the small motorcycle.

"Where do I put my pack?" she asked pointing to the bulky bag.

"Pack on," he said indicating to leave it on her shoulders. She was suddenly glad she had shipped home at least twenty pounds of gifts and gear so as not to tip over the bike. She climbed on feeling top heavy. When the motor zoomed to life she reflexively grabbed around the driver's waist. Without a smile he sped through streets and wove around pedestrians in the low-built city. There were no tall structures; buildings were three stories at most and store fronts were filled with adolescents and small children.

Maddy realized that they had not discussed a destination or a price and she leaned into the driver's ear and said "backpacker hotel, please." He must have already known because his course did not change and he slowed only slightly for corners, just enough so that she did not fly off. Maddy noticed that few people smiled as they walked or shopped and there were large numbers of men missing one or both legs. Rows of beggars clogged the street entrance near the market as the poor and disfigured vied for charity. The driver navigated the crowd and pushed up a small street. He stopped short in front of a blocky white building labeled Capital Guest House. European-looking travelers milled around, unloaded packs, and congregated next to the building to smoke.

Tiny white lights hung low along the doorway and Maddy's eyes flew open wide; she had completely forgotten it was the end of December.

"What is today?" she asked the driver.

"Twenty-three, December," the driver said.

"Christmas Eve is tomorrow," she exclaimed. She fumbled for her money pouch and produced a small stack of American bills. The driver accepted several, nodded, and sped off. She was greeted in the lobby by a woman's thick Asian accent which overlaid her broken English.

"Hello--one room, yes?" called the small woman behind the counter.

"Yes."

"You share?" she asked.

"No, I'm alone." Maddy replied.

"You share--I put you wit other girl."

"Oh sure, I can share a room." Maddy agreed. She was out of practice at booking a room. It hadn't occurred to her to request a room-share with another traveler, but that would be a great way to meet people. She took a key and turned right at the crooked artificial Christmas tree and went up the stairs. She was touched by the effort to make the Western travelers feel at home. Maddy opened the door to a small but clean room with two tiny bookshelves, two hooks, two chairs, and a bunk bed along the back wall. It looked like a miniature dorm room on the first day of college. She sighed at the empty room and put her pack on the bench and sat next to it. She didn't exactly miss Richard but she missed having company, knowing someone. No matter how difficult he had been, Richard had always been a form of company.

Maddy dug out her Cambodia guide book and leafed through it to see what Phnom Penh held in store. The history was tumultuous at best. It was not the original capital, which was located at Angkor during the height of the Khmer Empire. Phnom Penh was established as the capital in the fifteenth century and held its position for three hundred years. In 1834 it was burned down during a clash with the Siamese and the whole town was rebuilt during the French occupation in 1863. Many of the gardens and buildings in French colonial style still remained. The city gained independence from France in 1954 only to fall to the Khmer Rouge twenty years later. The Khmer Rouge was a brutal regime that exterminated most the Cambodian middle class, the intellectuals, and the artists of the time. The guide book encouraged travelers to be gentle and kind since most of the population was under thirty and still recovering from personal and cultural cataclysm.

Maddy read the section on getting around and decided she had better find a ticket to Siem Reap to see Angkor Wat. Out on the street she was accosted by a brigade of young motorcycle-taxi drivers and she nodded toward one. Drivers whizzed by with women sitting side saddle carrying grocery bags and baskets. Maddy got off at a tourist stop called Byron's Books. Byron was an American who, according to the guide book, had fought in Vietnam and had stayed in Southeast Asia ever since. He made himself a permanent fixture by starting a book and ticket shop which was the hub for backpacker travel in Cambodia.

The shop was just a shack with benches out front that looked out onto the bank of the Tonle Sap River. Grungy travelers filled the seats and read maps and wrote postcards in the humid afternoon. Inside, Byron was a crusty sort with a ruddy complexion. He pointed to the blackboard at the options for getting to Ankor.

"You can take a bus if you want, but I think the river is safer and more to see," he said.

"Safer how?" Maddy asked."

"Once in a while someone will hold up the bus and shake people down for money," Byron explained. "Course the river is not always one hundred percent either," he trailed off, and nodded to someone looking for the bathroom.

"Which one will get me there in one piece?" Maddy tried again.

Byron looked slightly annoyed and clarified his earlier statement, "Some old Khmer factions will occasionally shoot at the bus just to make a statement."

Maddy shook her head in a quandary; she always preferred a land route, but didn't want to get robbed or shot. Richard would have loved this. She ran through different scenarios in her head before being interrupted.

"Are ye gen to buy a ticket or not?" A tall muscular Irishman asked from behind her. He had straggly hair and looked as if he had not changed his clothes in a week. Not wanting to look like a coward or a nuisance, Maddy nodded and handed Byron a stack of American bills which he happily accepted.

He handed her a boat ticket. "Christmas at Angkor Wat," Bryon said. "Have fun."

Maddy stepped outside and immediately felt awkward.

At home, she and Richard traditionally had dinner with Caroline on Christmas Eve and then went to a movie on Christmas day. She sat down and opened her journal and stared at the following day, a blank date, December twenty four. Being solo during the holiday reminded her of when she'd stayed at college over a winter break and was the only person in the huge dorm. She had ordered pizza, had a bottle of wine, and dug into a good book. It had been lonely but she had survived and felt stronger for having done so. Devoid of any better ideas she stepped back into the bookstore and bought a brightly covered book that had, "Hilarious" written at the top of the reviews. She had the rest of the day to kill so she flagged down a driver and asked him to show her the sights of Phnom Penh.

"Thirty dollars, all day," he negotiated and they sped off in a cloud of smoke. They went to the National Museum in the center of the city just past the Royal Palace. The museum featured ancient Khmer art, Hindu statues and pottery that seemed too old to still be intact; some of the bronze pieces dated back to the fourth century. Next was a stop at the Royal Palace near the river banks built in 1813, which showcased beautiful landscaped grounds and a strange mix of French and Chinese designed buildings. It was as if someone had taken colonial buildings and replaced the roofs with pagoda-like caps. Inside, the décor was a mish-mosh of Buddhist and Hindu art. The only nod to Khmer history was the large pyramid-like obelisks made of concrete that were interspersed in the gardens. They were ornately carved and had the appearance of lattice-covered sand castles which towered above all the other statues.

Maddy read through the history section of her guidebook and concluded that like Cambodia in general, Phnom Penh was a confluence of the many cultures and people that had occupied, ruled, or rebuilt it; each one contributing a piece of itself to create a country. They stopped for a late lunch at a tiny hidden café that had no menus. The driver ordered what translated as Fish Amok, a national favorite dish of steamed fish inside banana leaves with curry, lemongrass, and chilies. Coconut and egg were added to form a soft custard around the tender fish. Tentative at first, Maddy was quickly won over by the velvet texture and zingy spice in each bite.

They made one more stop late in the afternoon at the Tuol Sleng Genocide Museum known as S-2, a former Khmer Rouge prison. It was a ghostly place with thousands of black and white photos of prisoners who were held, interrogated, and executed there. Rooms still had the small metal frame beds and chains used to hold people down during torture. The prison was said to have been left just as it was the day the Khmer were driven out by the Vietnamese in 1979.

Maddy wandered the stark halls filled with photos; black eyes stared out. A shiver ran over her even in the heat and she slumped on the back of the motor bike all the way back to the guesthouse. She thanked her driver for his hospitality.

The next morning was sticky and travelers gathered at the small dock along the river. Many languages, mostly European and various English dialects, could be distinguished among the chatter. Maddy never thought of Angkor Wat as a Christmas destination but the idea was exotic. She was getting used to being alone, making decisions without consult. But two questions hung in the back of her mind at all times: Where would she go after her money ran out? What was she going to do with her life after that? She pushed back the uncertainties that lay with both dilemmas and focused on catching the boat.

She was lost in thought when the boat motored up to the narrow dock. It looked like a submarine, bullet shaped and riding low in the water. A man gestured to board and backpacks were stored away on metal shelves at the back of the tubular cabin. It was hot inside. The porthole style windows only opened a few inches making the sub feel sticky and damp. Maddy found a seat and surveyed the riders. She recognized the young Irish man from Byron's Books. Today he was with two friends. Also, today his hair was freshly washed and his trousers, thought wrinkled from being crushed in a backpack, were clean. A thick shouldered man with blond hair and a New Zealand flag on his pack ducked in through the small round door and sat behind two Dutch women wearing red felt reindeer antlers. He smiled at their holiday cheer and struck up a lively conversation. A handful of other seats were filled by locals traveling from the capital to Siem Reap. The twenty-something captain collected tickets and maneuvered the tube into a U-turn heading up stream.

Maddy had read that the Tonle Sap River was a major tributary of the Mekong River. Due to snow melt in the Himalayas, the river would fill and back up to create a reservoir in the Mekong Delta, forcing the Tonle Sap to run backward during the rainy season. It was past that time so the river was moving in its normal direction as the boat pushed against the current toward Ankor. Maddy watched the muddy water part at the bow. The river seemed lifeless but occasionally a fisherman could be spotted from the bank pulling on a taut line.

Midway to Siem Reap while Maddy was listening to the Dutch-New Zealand conversation, the captain and his helper started exchanging quick words that sounded like the plucking of guitar strings. Their pitch grew high and fast and the Cambodian passengers pressed their faces to the windows and chattered rapidly. Maddy looked in the same direction but saw nothing but brown water lapping the banks on either side. The Irishmen, deep in conversation, didn't seem to notice the growing urgency of the men's voices until all at once the captain's helper shouted something in Cambodian. Maddy watched in confusion as people began to scramble about the metal tube. She grabbed her small bag and got up and moved toward the exit.

"Git daun, git daun," hollered the rumpled Irishmen as

he ran toward her. He tackled her and brought them both to the floor. He dragged her out of the isle between two seats and heaved with heavy breath.

"What the hell is going on?" Maddy pushed at him trying to look around.

"Ye stupid cow," he said. His brogue was so thick that it took several seconds to decipher his words. "Yer goen te get shot."

"Shot?" she said, then shrieked as a twangy crash of bullets slammed against the metal hull. She buried her face in the Irishmen's neck and clung to him as he fully covered her with his body. The boat captain was quick to reply, firing a burst of gunfire toward the bank and cranking the engine full speed to power upstream.

Maddy's breath heaved under the weight of the Irishman's body. His canvas cargo pants were laden with full pockets of odd shaped objects. As the cries in the cabin quieted, she guessed at the contents of his pockets--Swiss army knife in the right lower thigh, wallet in the left front. She was mildly crushed but very grateful for his protection and grew more and more aware of his musky scent and continuous pressure on her. His hair was still damp at the tips and he smelled of sage and hash, as if his shirt had been used to wrap and protect the herbs. As the boat slowed, he shifted his weight but Maddy held tight.

He looked down and smiled. "Fine, I'll keep ye here," he said and relaxed allowing all of him to press into her. It had been so long since she had been this close to anyone, more than a year, she tried to remember. Maybe two?

People started rising from the floor of the vessel and he looked at her again. "Oh, ok," she said. Before he scooted off her, he pressed his face close to her ear and said, "Me name is Duncan."

"Thanks for saving me--I'm Maddy." He helped her up and into a seat. Her face was flushed, ears burning red hot. He nodded at her with a small smile and ducked out the door to join his friends. She sat facing backward, shocked at the idea of being shot at and at the racing thoughts of Duncan, several years her junior. She had cloaked all sexual desire since Franz in Nepal and it emerged now in bounding palpitations that left her shaken; Duncan's scent rested with her. What are the rules, she wondered? Was she officially separated from Richard? She looked at her left hand, at the blank ring finger. Not that it mattered to some men but there was no outward indication of her status. She licked the taste of salty adrenalin from her lips and listened to the Dutch women talk in their native tongue as everyone on board began to relax. The boat moved steadily upstream.

Siem Reap was an old colonial town spread out between the Royal Independence Gardens at one end and the Old Market at the other. The market district was lined with guesthouses, bars, and shops to serve the influx of travelers all year. Travel agents competed to sell tickets to Angkor Wat, a World Heritage site and tourist Mecca of Cambodia.

All the backpackers on the boat had been buzzed to the market district and dropped off to find lodging. Maddy checked into Palin Guesthouse and was greeted by a short, friendly man who introduced himself as Mr. David. He showed her to a room that looked as though it was just out of a romantic movie. Gleaming dark hardwood floors led to teak benches inset at the window and a bed hung with a canopy-style lavender mosquito net. The draped net obscured tiny satin pillows embroidered with gold and purple threads. Maddy was overwhelmed by the lavish room after so many months of spare backpacker accommodation.

"Do you like it?" Mr. David asked.

"It's beautiful," she whispered. "Thank you."

She closed the door and removed her pack and spun in a circle taking in the rich smooth wood on the walls. It was impossible that this beautiful room was hers for only twenty U.S. dollars per night. She climbed beneath the netting and lay grinning on the harem-worthy bed. She giggled like a teenager at the idea of making love under the purple curtain. Duncan rose in her mind. She blushed and pressed her face into to a satin pillow. She tried to push the thought away but was reminded of the Rumi quote: 'Be Notorious.' Would this qualify? She quickly changed into clean clothes, grabbed her guide book and headed out to learn the town, all the while keeping an eye out for Duncan.

Angkor Wat, translated as the city of temples, was the largest Hindu complex in the world. It was built in the 12th century and was once the capital of the Khmer empire. The outer walls contained more than two hundred acres of grounds and temples. The perimeter was surrounded by a rectangular moat. The central temple had multiple galleries each rising above the next toward the highest center peak originally dedicated to the Hindu god Vishnu, but was later converted to Theravada Buddhism. The tower stood sixty five meters high and Maddy stared at the intricate structure. It was flanked at the corners by four additional sandstone temples shaped like soft serve ice cream cones draped in a lacy pattern of carvings. A narrow staircase led upward as if climbing to the sky and the shallow steps were steep. Maddy read that they represented the arduous journey of ascending toward the gods. She walked the perimeter of the central complex running her fingers along carvings of animals and dancers shown in contorted postures. She relished the luxury of time and quiet here. She savored the slow exploration of this fantastic place, taking time to read, sit, and rest.

In the afternoon she took the stairs to the top of the central tower to look out over Siem Reap. It stretched along the snaking Mekong River and butted up against a dense forest at Ankor. After a leisurely walk along the moat, she caught a bus back into town for dinner. The Dutch women from the boat were walking in the main part of town and invited Maddy to join them for dinner. They ate fried fish at a local vendor then slipped next door to a bar for drinks. By dusk the sky was lit by a saffron glow. A full moon rose over the river. Maddy suddenly thought again of the central tower in Angkor Wat and knew she had to see the moon from there. She thanked the women and zipped back to the hotel to retrieve her coat. After a quick hello to Mr. David she flagged down a motor taxi and buzzed out to the central Angkor temple.

The lights above the moat illuminated the bridge like a runway through the outer wall then fell to shadow from the moon. The rosebud-cone-shaped temple peaks blocked out most of the moonlight. Maddy dragged her hand along the walls until she found the long ascending staircase in the main temple. The air grew cool and pushed out the humidity of the earlier day. Maddy picked her way up the rough stairs of the center temple and climbed high over the courtyard. Balanced in the onyx sky, the full moon hung seemingly inches away. It filled her completely with its perfect roundness. Not since the Himalayas had she felt so close to such bewitching beauty. She felt around for the short walled platform and found a seat facing east. She sat down to watch the lunar ascent.

On her first Christmas Eve alone, Maddy felt both blessed and lonely. She knew that this could mark the beginning of solo holidays for her and she also knew that she was very fortunate to be in this sacred historical site for Christmas Eve. A breeze brushed at her cooling skin.

Christmas morning Maddy awoke to the exotic purple netting that swaddled the bed. She tiptoed to the door and smiled at the breakfast tray left there by Mr. David. Boiled eggs, toast and jam were accompanied by a candy cane tied to a napkin. She ate breakfast and decided to stay for the rest of the week to relax and explore more of the temples. Besides seeing the sights, she hoped to see Duncan again.

Maddy asked around about a guide and was introduced to Nhean. He was twenty-something with a big grin and even bigger sunglasses. He spoke slang English and was happy to show Maddy around Angkor. They started at Angkor Thom temple, which housed The Bayon, a collection of 216 identical sculpted faces. History told that King Jayavarman VII had built the faces during his reign, perhaps to intimate to his people that they were being watched. The twenty foot genderless faces were carved four to a pillar looking out in all directions so that no matter where you stood, you couldn't escape their watchful eyes. Maddy wandered the reconstructed garden ruins and admired the Khmer statues; some whole despite being thousands of years old, some fractured like the history of the country.

The next day she and Nhean traveled forty miles out of Siem Reap to the temple of Banteay Srei. Ornately carved red sandstone statues, walls, and alcoves made up the temple dedicated to the Hindu god Shiva. Its tightly clustered structures and embellished carvings created the feeling of being in a maze and Maddy made sure to keep Nhean close by. They tromped around stirring up red dust with each step. When they had seen all the temple grounds, they motored back to the main Angkor temple to see the sun set over the rectangular pools. By the end of the week, Maddy had covered all of the major temples and sights of

Siem Reap. She felt satisfied at having taken the time to really see all she wanted. She would never have spent an entire week had Richard been there.

She sat in the guesthouse garden and plopped her guidebook on the table. A map, loaned to her by Mr. David, was spread open and Maddy munched on French bread and worked on a travel plan.

"Going somewhere?" a voice said.

A blush outpaced her smile and rose high on her cheeks when the deep Irish accent registered. "Where have you been all week?" Maddy asked.

"In the jungle," he said, "looking for some ruins." His cargo pants hung low and he wore a Cambodia tee shirt found at every tourist kiosk in town. Maddy forced herself to shift her gaze back up to his eyes.

"Ye kent leave on New Year's Eve." Duncan smiled and sat down.

"You have plans?" She asked.

This time he blushed a shade of strawberry that highlighted his curls. He shrugged. "Me and mey sham are goen to find some bevvies and music--want to come?"

"Yeah, why not," Maddy accepted. "Sounds fun."

"Good, good, then I'll knock you round at half nine." He gave her hand a quick squeeze and ambled out into the street.

She laughed at the idiom and at her own giddy giggle that bubbled up like a teenager asked to prom. The feeling only lasted for a second, as she reminded herself she was only weeks out of a long marriage. She pushed away the thought of her wonky marital status. She vowed to herself not to worry about the outcome or the consequences; she was just going to have a few drinks with a couple of traveling Irishmen.

She finished looking at the map and writing a postcard to Caroline, then gathered her things to go in search of a post office. Suddenly, she thought of Diya and wished she had an address for her. It was foolish really, Maddy had only known her for a few days, but the intensity of their meeting had laid down a ribbon in Maddy's memory. She wondered if Diya had gone back to pick up Aarush by now. Maybe she had just gone home to talk to her father first. Maddy shook her head at the complexity of such a problem. She put aside the heavy thoughts for the time being. She stopped inside to tell Mr. David that she was going to spend at least one more night in town, maybe two.

Freshly showered and dressed in a silk-flowered tank, Maddy waited outside until she heard the Irish trio coming up the street. Holding her breath, she popped out to meet them.

"Hey, this is Brenden and Sean," Duncan said. They all shook hands before setting off to find a lively place to hang out. In bar after bar, the lights were bright and music tumbled out into the street. They chose a bar playing loud classic rock. Duncan hollered in her ear, "What are ye drinking tonight?"

"Gin and tonic," she shouted back.

They retreated to a small table. She sipped on the popping bubbles that jumped from the tall plastic cup. Duncan, Sean, and Brenden pounded back one pitcher of beer, then another. She enjoyed their teasing exchange, only understanding a portion because of the accent and Irish slang.

"Ye need a bazzer," Sean scuffed at Duncan's head. Duncan ducked almost out of the way, loose curls swinging on his forehead.

"What's a bazzer?" Maddy asked.

"A haircut," Sean explained. "Duncan doesn't like to cut off his curls."

"As well he shouldn't," Maddy replied, drawing a whistle from Brenden.

"Maybe she'll give ye a bob," Brenden said. Duncan landed a fist on his shoulder.

"Never mind," Duncan said turning to Maddy, "let's dance."

He grabbed her hand, pulled her close, and pulsed to the music despite Maddy's embarrassed laugh. Brenden wiggled between other dancers and handed Maddy another tall gin and tonic before gyrating away into the crowd. She gulped down two deep slurps before meeting eyes with Duncan again. The gin warmed her insides. The song changed to Hungry Like the Wolf by Duran Duran. Maddy laughed out loud. The song was popular years ago in the states, but was just now coming into the fashion in

Cambodia.

Backpackers, ex-pats and locals pressed into the bar and filled the dance floor in a crush of people ready to ring in the New Year. Duncan, with great skill, danced with one hand around a beer and the other around Maddy. He pulled her close when the beat intensified and spun her on tempo change. As midnight approached, people sang loud and free having long surpassed normal alcohol levels. Brenden had come by once more to ply Maddy with gin and refresh Duncan's beer. When the countdown to midnight began, both Maddy and Duncan had a stack of empty plastic cups in hand. At the stroke of the clock and call of the DJ, everyone threw their cups into the air shouting Happy New Year! Duncan, now with both hands free clasped Maddy in a dramatic dip and kissed her. It was a long sweet kiss with more finesse than seemed possible after so much beer. She felt heat rise in her belly as when he had held her down on the boat. His lips parted to offer her more. She surrendered to his encircled arms, letting doubt and fear drain from her mind.

"Let's go," he whispered onto her lips.

They wove through the crowd out to the cooler air in the street. She was thankful for the arm he kept around her waist as they teetered down the street. She leaned into him all the way back to her room.

Mr. David was already in bed and the guesthouse was quiet. She tried to be silent as she tip-toed across the gleaming wood floor. Inside her room, Duncan pressed her against the closed door with a fiery kiss and then backed her onto the purple draped bed. They fell back with a thump and laughed at the crash landing. Maddy kicked her feet free of the mosquito net. Duncan sprinkled kisses on her neck and shoulders, light as a butterfly, leaving goose bumps in their wake. He hovered over her easily holding his weight up on lean arms. Her fingers outlined the shape of his muscles. She could feel the long dampened fire inside her spark to life. The gin tried to drown out the small, dark doubt that was always with her, and as the alcohol wore off, worry was there like a toothache. Maddy watched, mostly out of body as Duncan unbuttoned her shirt and moved soft lips toward her belly; his hands capturing her breasts. She would have to make a decision quickly in order to stop him but the idea filled her with fatigue.

"I'll be right back," he said and kissed her navel before ducking out of the tented bed. She was hazy and heavy and gazed at the filmy net not believing that the moment was real. The exotic warmth of the bed engulfed her and she breathed deeply of the scent left behind by his lithe body. She felt the netting rise and then fall and she fell into the warmth.

Maddy awoke to slits of light cutting through the window blinds to lay a fence pattern across the bed. Her mouth was as thick as her head and she felt a dull pain behind her eyes. She reached next to her in search of Duncan's body but found only an empty space of wrinkled sheet. She opened her eyes and saw that she was still wearing her socks and pants, although her shirt was missing. Where was Duncan, had she dreamed the whole encounter?

"I need coffee," she said and the vibration of her voice made her temples throb. She found her shirt and gently cracked the door. She was greeted by a cheerful good morning from Mr. David whose voice rattled off the hardwood floor.

"Hello--by chance do you have some coffee?" She asked. He nodded and returned with a creamy, steaming cup.

"Did you have fun at the American New Year?" He asked. She looked at him through one eye and wondered how he had come to being called Mr. David.

"Did you see my friend leave?" She decided that her need to know outweighed any potential embarrassment.

"Oh yes, last night--after midnight. He brought you in and left a while later."

Maddy nodded in thanks; part of her relieved, part disappointed.

She slid the door shut, her forehead resting on the graceful old wood. What am I doing? The question made her leaden with fatigue and she curled up on the bed in an attempt to avoid her confusion. An hour went by without answer and she concluded that Duncan's leaving had actually spared her. She wasn't sure how to negotiate an established relationship let alone a new sexual one. She didn't know what her life was about just then, but was sure that hopping into bed with a young Irishmen was not going to make things any simpler.

Her hair was wet and the air was warm in the French bakery that enticed occupants with the fresh scent of yeasty bread. She stood in line for more coffee and a hot baguette and read the 'getting there' section of the Vietnam travel guide.

"Leaving again?" The words pressed close to her neck.

Maddy turned right into Duncan's arms and his lips pressed against hers. "Happy New Year--again."

Her heart thumped so loud she was sure to have to yell over the noise. "Where did you go last night?"

"Ye knew?" he said. "I thought you were out for the din."

"Mr. David said you left last night after bringing me in."

He brushed a strand of hair off her face. "Ye were fast asleep when I came back from the jacks; you were bolloxed."

"You are quite the gentleman," she blushed.

"I was buckled meself, but not so as to take off yer cacks while you sleep."

"Thank you--I suppose--maybe I wanted my cacks off," she smiled. He kissed her cheek and they grabbed a small table.

"I'm off to Saigon tomorrow if I can get a ticket," she said.

"Aw--it's a hell of a place--I loved it," he said.

She stared at his youthful face, spirited with clear blue eyes, and once again felt the tug of war inside of her between desire and reason.

"If yer not leaving till the morrow, I can come round tonight." He punctuated the words with a tiny inflection.

She was afraid he would make that offer. She took his hand and leveled with him.

"You have no idea how enticing that offer is, but I think my oh-so-attractive passing out last night probably saved me from myself," she sighed.

"What holds ye back?" He asked.

"The fact that I'm sort of technically married-- separated at least."

His eyes bounded open but he did not withdraw his hand.

"Where's yer husband?" He asked.

"I don't know. Last time I saw him was in India." The butter on her plate suddenly looked waxy and too yellow. She flicked a bit of bread crumb off her lap.

"What happened?" Duncan asked.

Maddy shrugged. "We didn't get on much, even at home. I thought traveling would help, but it just got worse. Then I cracked, and ran--literally."

"Are ye never goin to see him again?"

"I don't know. Eventually I'll have to go home and sign papers."

"I ken the problem." He stole a bite of bread off her

plate and she watched his soft pink tongue lick shiny butter from his lips. He broke into a wide slippery grin. "Well if ye figure it straight by tonight, come ring me round." He got up and kissed her cheek leaving a buttery smudge. She watched him saunter out of the café.

Fourteen

It was noon when she awoke from a nap somewhere
between Cambodia and Vietnam. It had been a bumpy ride
for the first few hours toward Saigon before she had fallen
asleep, but fatigue from drinking and the night of moral
wrestling had taken its toll. The sun stood high over the
bus with no shadows on either side. The cabin was only
partially full and travelers had their backpacks in seats
next to them like dusty companions decorated in buckles
and straps. A grey haired woman in a lavender shirt sat
across from Maddy and read a travel guide for Vietnam.
Maddy leaned over to glimpse the woman's pack in hopes
of determining where she was from. The woman looked up
and smiled.

"Hello." Her accent was light; British? Australian?
Kiwi?

"Hi," Maddy said. "Are you going to Saigon?"

"You mean Ho Chi Min City?" She smiled a row of
white Chicklet teeth.

"Yes, I forgot it is called that." Maddy replied. "Do you
know when we are supposed to arrive?"

"Another several hours to the border, then we have to

get a ride from there."

"Really?" The travel agent in Siem Reap said nothing about the bus ending at the border, though it made sense, since technically it was an international crossing. "I guess I'd better read up on how to get into the city." Maddy said.

"Where are you from?" The woman asked.

"The US. You?"

"Australia. My name is Louisa." She bent around to offer a petite hand.

"I'm Maddy--nice to meet you. Are you traveling alone?"

"For a bit, yea. I did a trek in Burma, then over to Ankor for New Year. I'm meeting my boyfriend in a few days and we will travel together through Vietnam."

"He didn't want to go to Burma with you?" Maddy asked.

Louisa shook her head. "Yes, but he couldn't get the time off until now. What about you, traveling solo?"

Maddy sighed. "It's a long story."

"Well--we have several hours...." Louisa was small and wiry. Her silver hair pooled around her shoulders. She cocked her head to listen to Maddy's story.

The trip to the border seemed short as they shared travel stories, best reads, places to avoid, and relationship woes. Maddy was again amazed at the instant intimacy. It was as if they might only know one another for a day, so it made sense to skip all the formality and dive right into the middle. Maybe it was also the fact that if Maddy never saw

Louisa again then the risk was removed; no judgment, no feedback, no worry.

Maddy shared her story of running away from Richard at the Amber Fort.

"It's quite symbolic really," Louisa said. "You were in a place of supposed safety only to feel trapped and compelled to find freedom--remove all obstacles--as Ganesh represents."

"That's true," Maddy said. "But what now? I'm just wandering around not sure where to go or what to do."

"Don't worry, you will figure it out. You will know when you know." Louisa smiled.

The bus slowed at a wide spot in the road about one hundred yards from a colossal pagoda structure over the roadway. It had spikey letters that might have said Welcome in Vietnamese but looked more Chinese than anything else. There was no one there; no customs office or border guards, no restaurants or bathrooms. The bus driver stood and waved for people to get off the bus. Maddy looked at Louisa, who shrugged and disembarked with the other passengers. The driver chucked out several backpacks and a large trunk from the cargo storage beneath the bus, closed the door, and drove off.

"This is a joke right?" Maddy said aloud.

Birds circled above the anemic forest on either side of road. From where the bus had just left came a buzz from off in the distance and the small group strained to look. A dust cloud rose and obscured the source of the noise momentarily. The curtain of dust was pierced by a pack of motor bikes. Ten bikes in all raced directly at the travelers who stood in the center of the road. The bikes split like choreographed circus riders and circled the group.

"This is bad," said a middle-aged man with the large trunk. The riders drove round and round as though herding cattle and kicked up a funnel cloud in the clearing.

"What do we do?" Maddy yelled over the noise of the two stroke engines.

"Run for the border crossing," yelled the man as he abandoned his huge trunk and shot through an opening between two motorcycles in a full sprint toward the pagoda. Maddy tried to cut through but was herded by a driver that guarded her using a tight zone defense. The motorbikes circled and circled. Finally one stopped. The driver, wearing huge sunglasses and a baseball cap pulled low on his forehead, got off and approached the group. He pointed toward Louisa's small travel bag and motioned for money. He didn't grab at the bag but waited for her to open the purse. He looked at each person in turn. A weary faced couple quickly dug out a stack of US dollars and some Cambodian Rial and handed them over. Louisa didn't budge. She unbuckled her purse and shoved it deep into her pants. The mugger was young and had a small, wiry frame but was still bigger than Louisa by inches. But Louisa didn't flinch and appeared ready to strike like a cobra. Maddy followed suit and shoved her bum bag down into her pants. It bulged like a tumor growing from her groin. She stood next to Louisa and tried to appear tough. Heartbeats pounded in her ears and drowned out the circling motors. The man yelled something to his gang but his voice was lost in the roar.

In one swift move Louisa grabbed Maddy's hand and yelled: "Now!" They bolted off in a dead run toward the pagoda border as fast as they could under the weight of full backpacks. Motor bikes scattered in an effort to herd them back but the other travelers also sprinted, spreading out in all directions. The gang tried but failed to re-circle the group. Just then, a car raced forward from underneath the pagoda. In the passenger seat was the older man who had run free first. He had found a cab on the other side and had returned to retrieve his trunk. The cab driver barreled at the motorcycles like a sport, weaving and chasing them. He spun the small car in a circle to charge again. By the third pass the motorcycle gang swirled off down the road and the cabdriver pulled up next to the man's trunk and loaded it in the boot of the car. The backpackers huddled beyond the pagoda panting and spitting dirt.

"Holy crap, chick--you are brave." Maddy said to Louisa.

"Not really, I just figured it was worth a try. He didn't look prepared to force the issue. Besides I have been robbed once already this trip and I wasn't about to give up my cash again."

Maddy laughed. "Well thanks, I didn't really want to be mugged either."

The man, now reunited with his trunk, gestured to the remaining seats in his cab.

"You guys go." Maddy said to the shaken young couple who had handed over their money. She and Louisa turned and started walking down the road toward Saigon.

They hadn't walked far when another cab whizzed up and offered them a ride for an extortionist rate. Maddy shrugged, "at least we get something for our money other than a mouthful of dirt."

Rice paddies bordered the road most of the way. Some were green with new sprouts while other looked like flooded plains. Oxen harnessed with dense wooden yokes pulled sickle shaped plows through the muddy terrain. It looked straight out of The Good Earth. Maddy watched the landscape turn from rural to urban as the taxi approached Ho Chi Minh City. It was strange to be heading into a city defined in American culture by a hideous war. Maddy wondered what the Vietnamese thought of Americans and she wished, not for the first time, that she had a Canadian flag on her pack. How should she act in a culture invaded by her home country that left a generation of people dead or damaged?

Ho Chi Minh City was a city under construction. Buildings were flanked by scaffolding and dust filled the air. The taxi deposited them in a busy part of town filled with hotels and cheap backpacker restaurants. Maddy looked around at the street side cafes which overflowed with tourists. She concluded that every twenty-something of European descent was essentially eating and drinking their way around the globe. Open air tables were packed with grungy traveler's playing cards, writing postcards, and plotting routes on world maps. It had become a familiar scene and she felt strangely at home.

"Let's get a hotel." Louisa headed toward a clean-ish looking place.

"When does your boyfriend arrive?" Maddy asked.

"Not until tomorrow, so we can book in together until then." Louisa said.

After a shower and change of clothes, Maddy and Louisa collapsed into the last booth at the Sing Café across the street. They had just started on coffee when a handsome, dark haired man and a tall lean woman arrived and scoured the café for a seat. Not finding an empty booth they gestured to the two open places beside Maddy and Louisa.

"Join us." Louisa offered and the man squeezed in next to Maddy.

"Hello, I'm Giovanni." He offered his hand. His fingers were soft and feather light. The woman spoke in a thick Dutch accent and introduced herself as Aletta.

"Are you traveling together?" Maddy asked.

"No, we have met only a day before," Aletta said. "When did you arrive?"

"Just a few hours ago, after a fashion." Louisa said. She pushed silver-grey strands of hair away from her cup.

"Some excitement already?" Giovanni questioned with

a smile. "What happened?"

"We got held up at the border by some would-be robbers." Maddy explained.

"Did they take your passports?" Aletta asked.

"No, they wanted money," Louisa laughed. "I stuck my purse down my pants and refused to hand it over."

Giovanni whistled. "So small and so brave. And you?" He looked at Maddy.

"Ditto. They didn't get a thing from me either." High fives rose above the table. "That deserves a toast," Giovanni said.

"It's only two o'clock." Maddy laughed.

"Ok, maybe later," he said.

After lunch Maddy and Louisa wandered toward the Jade Emperor Pagoda. It was hailed in the guidebooks as a must-see in Ho Chi Minh City. They walked along dusty streets and Louisa sprang a question on Maddy.

"How are you doing since your marriage fell apart? It's only been a few weeks?" Louisa asked.

Maddy's spirit fell like Saigon in 1975. Her feet slowed and shoulders slumped as her barely suppressed dilemma surfaced again. "Part of me feels like it was a lifetime ago. Eventually I'll have to go home and face reality. What if when I get home I realize I've made a mistake?"

"Don't look at me," Louisa said. "I've been with Aaden for nine years and I'm never sure."

"He doesn't want to get married?" Maddy asked.

"No," Louisa said. "Just the opposite - I don't want to get married. He has asked several times and I just can't say yes."

"Why? What stops you?" Maddy was curious. All of her friends back home were either married or trying to find someone to marry.

"I was married before when I was young like you. I love Aaden but I don't like the whole institution of marriage"

"Don't you feel alone or isolated at times?" Maddy asked.

"Sure, when I travel alone or get off a plane in a new place. Life has an infinite supply of lonely landings, but it's also full of joy and beauty and kindness. It's all about finding yourself and accepting the rest." Louisa's Aussie twang made it sound so easy.

Maddy looked at her feet. "I guess I was so focused on being married that I never figured out what my own life was about."

"Yes, sometimes we get off track. But you seem to be on your way now." Louisa stopped in front of a huge red Chinese structure.

"I thought it was jade," Maddy said.

Louisa shook her head and smiled. "It's named after the Jade Emperor, not the stone." Maddy's cheeks turned pink. They purchased tickets and wandered around the structured gardens and Maddy considered her life. Back home she had a house, an unremarkable job, no children, and no achievements to speak of. Yes, she was traveling and seeing the world, but what did that mean? What wisdom would she take home?

"What kind of work do you do?" Maddy asked Louisa.

"I work for a refugee aid agency. Mostly in Africa, but sometimes in other places. It's hard work at times, but never boring. I help set up temporary housing or site hospitals. I coordinate food deliveries. It can be heart breaking to see how much help people need, but I wouldn't trade it for any other work."

Maddy sat down on a short stone wall. She was dwarfed by a statue entitled: The Pure Ones; a triptych of ancient Chinese characters representing the past, present, and future. Her past was a life of superficiality; culturally mandated pursuits of college, marriage, and children. She seemed to have been moving through her life with little thought. She had no anchor in religion, no awareness of calling or passion. The present was certainly more interesting. Filled with history and culture, her present offered up a buffet of places and people. She was seeing things that few people in the world had the privilege of seeing: The Taj Mahal, the Ganges River, Ankor Wat, and the Himalayas. And yet she still felt like a passive observer. Leaving Richard was the most active life decision she had ever made. She was learning to be less fearful (except for flying). Interesting people were everywhere. Despite the good feeling of meeting other people, there remained an empty place inside her, a place that craved for meaning and purpose. Maddy looked at the third Chinese character representing the future. What did she want her future to look like?

"That's perfect," Louisa said. "I'll take your picture by the pure ones. Someday you will look back at this and smile."

That night, Maddy lay in the dark and listened to Louisa breathe and thought about the people who had touched her life in the past months: Helmar, Galiana, and Sebastian. Chrissy, Jack, Franz, Frederick, Simon and Rose, Ethan, and Louisa. Each person offered up a bit of personal wisdom. Several had shown compassion to her when she had struggled. All represented something she yearned for: a purpose. Each person seemed to give back to the world in some positive way. Maddy knew she must find a focus, a calling to give her direction and intent. It might not be grand like volunteering for the Red Cross, but something that would challenge her to be less self-centered and more deeply engaged in the world. She fell asleep while running ideas through her mind.

The Sing Café was already buzzing by the time Maddy and Louisa arrived. Hot French bread was rolling out of the kitchen. Louisa dug into a loaf and licked the butter off her fingers. Maddy popped a bite in her mouth and was bumped by the arrival of Giovanni who slid into the booth next to her.

"Ciao belle." His lips were plump and rose colored. One slightly crooked tooth made him look mischievous. Giovanni eyed the plate of hot bread and asked, "What are you ladies doing today?"

Louisa scooted the plate toward him with her pinky. He took a slab of bread, dredged it thick with butter, and hummed when he put it in his mouth.

"Fantastico," he pronounced.

"We're headed to the Reunification Palace today," Maddy said. "Want to come?"

"Why not. I was there last week so I can be your tour guide," he said.

Reunification Palace had been the presidential residence from 1966 until 1975 and was called Independence Hall until the day Saigon fell to the North Vietnamese. It was an oddly modern building, wide and flat with a huge bank of street-facing windows. The flag of Vietnam, deep red with a central gold star, flew at the top center of the building. Below the large flag was a row of smaller ones that lined a circular driveway. The palace had been left just as it stood in 1975 with beautifully decorated sitting rooms and chandeliered conference halls. Two commemorative tanks sat on the manicured lawn and made for a popular photo spot. Maddy and Louisa stood below the protruding gun barrel for Giovanni to snap a picture.

"It's so weird that the tourism here is based on a terrible war." Maddy said.

"Well, it's not unlike visiting Civil War sites in your own country," Louisa countered. "People want to learn more about the history."

Giovanni stood next to the tank treads. His pants hung

low on narrow hips. "Why did you come to Vietnam?" he asked Maddy.

"It's a long story." Maddy and Louisa said at the same time.

"Excellent, then tonight we will have dinner and wine and hear the whole tale." Giovanni said.

Aaden arrived late that afternoon and the four of them congregated at New World Hotel for dinner. It was a popular upscale place occupied by ex-pats and business men. Aaden was a full-blooded Aussie; blond, boisterous, and charming in a carefree way. He shook hands with Giovanni and hugged Maddy before settling down close to Louisa for the evening. Giovanni ordered a bottle of red wine, a seafood plate and rice noodles for all to share. They listened to Aaden's baggage woes while in Kuala Lumpur and how he now only had two pair of clean underwear to his name. Of the group, Giovanni had been traveling the longest and commented that two pair of underwear was a bounty, especially if they were both clean at the same time. He shared tales of going commando for days in India before figuring out how the laundry service worked. Maddy shared her story of the monkeys who stole her clothes from the balcony and they all laughed to tears.

After several glasses of wine, Giovanni turned to Maddy and said, "So Maddy we want to hear why you came to Vietnam."

Maddy winced. Louisa said, "It will get easier every time you tell it."

Maddy started in Europe and went up through Egypt when she had fallen ill. She explained about her challenges with Richard in Nepal and the idea of running away with Franz. Another bottle of wine was ordered and Giovanni filled glasses again while Maddy divulged her tale of escape in India and how she returned to Bangkok alone.

"Will you go back to him?" Giovanni asked.

"No. But I will have to go home and deal with the house and the divorce."

"Do you wonder where he is?" Aaden asked.

"Sometimes," Maddy replied. "It's weird not knowing."

"Well, we are all glad that you are here now," Louisa said.

"With that," Aaden said, "we are off to bed." He hugged an arm around Louisa's narrow frame and she raised her eyebrows. "Thanks for moving out of the room, Maddy." They waved goodnight.

"More wine?" Giovanni asked. Maddy grew quiet and accepted another glass.

Giovanni patted her hand. "It will all work out just the way it is supposed to." She smiled hoping he was right.

"Grazie mille," Maddy said in the little Italian she knew.

She woke early with a headache and an urge to move on. That second bottle of wine still haunted her. She stumbled across the street for coffee and found Louisa and Aaden already eating. She joined them for a bite and was happy to see their sleepy eyes stealing intimate glances back and forth. It was nice to see people in love. After breakfast Maddy thanked Louisa for a wonderful introduction to Vietnam and said goodbye. She grabbed a motor cab to the train station.

Muggy air filled the station as people gathered and Maddy was thankful when the train arrived and departed on time. Cracked vinyl covered the perfunctory bench seats in the coach. She found an empty seat next to a window. Rice paddies passed along the rolling terrain and thick forests leapt from nowhere then disappeared as quickly. Blasts of heat filled the coach every time the door opened and Maddy grew sleepy with the swaying of the train. She was about to fall asleep when another waft of heat moved in and Giovanni plopped down next to her.

"Oh my god--I didn't know you were leaving today." Maddy said.

"Must be fate," he wiggled his eyebrows. "Louisa told me you were leaving, so I thought I would join you."

"Well, thank you for arranging dinner last night, it was great fun."

"It was nothing and besides I got to hear your story."

"Yes, but I still don't know your story." Maddy turned to him. "What is your travel tale?"

"Ah, my tale has much excitement and danger, but it too is a long story."

"We have four hours on this train, so start talking,"

Maddy said.

Giovanni was from Bari, a port town on the east side of Italy where boats came and went mostly from Greece. His parents owned a small restaurant frequented by backpackers and tourists. People came from all over the world to see Italy; to admire the churches, visit museums, and to eat the fantastic food. Travelers who stopped at the family restaurant while on vacation loved to share their lives with the eager young Giovanni while he helped serve up pasta, and cannolis. In high school he saved all his earnings and dreamed of the places he wanted to see. While his peers bought clothes and scooters, he squirreled away his earnings into a savings account and waited for high school to end. Graduation finally came and he was about to launch his own travel dreams, when his mother, Isabella, fell ill.

"I knew it was cancer the morning she did not get up for coffee," he recounted as if in a trance. "She became so frail and weak it was awful to watch." He could not leave to travel, but at the insistence of both parents, he went to college in nearby Naples to study engineering at University of Frederico II. He hated it at first, saw no passion in modern structures but became enamored with a beautiful philosophy professor. He quickly changed his major to spend time with her. On weekends he went home to see his mother and over several years, she began to improve. The treatment left her without hair, which only made her eyes more beautiful. He was relieved to see her grow stronger.

In his third year, he concluded his affair with the professor but had fallen in love with philosophy and finished his degree before returning home. His father was running the restaurant alone without complaint, but was tired from burning the candle at both ends. He was happy to have his son home. Again, Giovanni delayed his travel plans. He stepped in to help his father and to pester his mother back to health. Isabella rallied under his attention, gained back her weight and her beautiful hair.

"She was so beautiful," he reminisced. "I've never known such a couple in love as my parents." His eyes grew moist.

"What happened?" Maddy prompted.

Giovanni pressed his eyes closed and his shoulders shook silently as a sob worked its way from his heart. He breathed hot air in gasps. After several minutes the tsunami of grief moved on. His body began to relax.

"My father fed everyone at the restaurant: fisherman, house cleaners, and wealthy business men. They came for the food and the family," Giovanni said.

After his mother returned to working in the restaurant, his father hosted a party for some Mafioso. An argument broke out between two men and they began pushing and smashing things on the table. Giovanni grabbed Isabella and ran back to the kitchen while his father tried to break up the fight.

"Glass smashed over and over and men wrestled and shouted, locked in anger like pit bulls. Amazingly, no one pulled a gun," Giovanni said. "I was torn between rushing out to help my father, and protecting my mother."

There was a huge crash as if a wall had come down, and then the banquet room cleared. It was silent. Giovanni waited for endless minutes listening for his father's voice, but nothing came. His mother tore free from his arms and ran into the banquet room. The dusty chandelier was swinging and his father Gino was lying next to the table. There was no blood, no bullets. But Gino's head rested at an unnatural angle.

Giovanni stopped again and covered his face with bony hands. Creases around his eyes crushed in grooves of anguish and a low moan escaped through his fingers. Maddy put an arm around his shoulders and held him like a child. Slowly, his pain abated with the rocking train.

"I'll never forget the sound that came from my mother. It was like a feral cat being torn apart by hyenas. Her howl filled the whole restaurant. She never really recovered. She went to bed and died within a year."

Giovanni sat, gutted by his story, and rested his head against the seat, eyes closed. They rode in silence for many miles up the coastline of Vietnam. Eventually Maddy said, "How long have you been traveling now?" He did not answer. Wet lashes formed tiny black spikes over his closed eyes. Minutes later Maddy realized he had fallen asleep.

Outside of Hoi An, the train slowed to a crawl. Women on bicycles peddled beside the train. The colorful tails of Vietnamese Ao dai flew behind them as they rode and traditional cone-shaped hats shaded their faces. Giovanni woke. He smiled and pointed to an old man carrying a long pole across his shoulders with chickens balanced on either side. Rice paddies were flooded knee deep and hosted groups of people bending low to plant fresh green sprigs.

Hoi An was a small town noted for local artists and robust open air markets. Maddy and Giovanni got separate rooms in the same guesthouse that had a common room filled with books and games left by travelers and ex-pats passing through. They walked down to the market after washing up and strolled through the vendor stalls. She noticed that some women wore western style clothes while others wore loose traditional dresses in soft colors. Fruits and vegetables in every shape and size overflowed the market tables.

"Those look so phallic," Giovanni said and pointed to some type of gourd and nudged Maddy's side. She smiled in agreement. The riverbank bustled with narrow boats that slid past one another in tiny slices of water to load or unload produce, chickens, or passengers. Bouncy Vietnamese vowels skipped across the water and filled the air. Unlike India, the locals seemed indifferent to tourists and went about their commerce.

In the cool night air they settled for dinner on the outdoor patio at the Lucky Luck restaurant. Despite the clear day, the night smelled like rain. Maddy ordered a tofu stir fry after glancing at the fish heads bobbing in broth. Some type of fish-ball soup was popular at the street vendor's stalls and she did not want to take a chance of ordering something inedible. Slick rice noodles in dark sauce came piled high with veggies and tofu. Giovanni dove into the mound with wooden chop sticks.

He didn't bother to clear his mouth before he spoke. "What happened to your marriage, I mean before you actually left?" Slick noodles dripped from his lips.

Maddy almost choked at the suddenness of his question. She had only known Giovanni for a week but one thing was very clear about him, he had a way of diving directly into the heart without fanfare or pretense. He was genuinely interested in everyone and in knowing the deeper part of every story. Tears pricked in her eyes before she could even formulate words.

"It was probably over as soon as it started, but I was too naïve to know better," Maddy said. "We lost a baby. He drank too much. We stopped having sex early on." It felt strangely like a lifetime ago.

"Your husband was a fool." Giovanni said.

"Is," she said. "He is still my husband. I think I'm still traveling to avoid going home to face the music. Besides, I don't really know what I want to do with my life."

"You have a passion? Something you love back home?" He asked.

"Not really. I had never given it any thought until this trip. I have met so many people doing amazing things, helping others, or just living a life full of meaning." She smiled remembering the tranquil life of Helmar and

Galiana. "I don't know what will happen next."

After dinner they walked and listened to the sounds of Hoi An. Merchants called out shoppers in their springy tones. Boats shuttled in the dark water. The sky, now deep blue, grew dense and heavy with the smell of moisture.

"I think it's going to rain," Giovanni said just as the rain began to fall. He grabbed her hand and ran through the streets under thick raindrops. They made it back to the guesthouse as the full weight of storm came down.

Hoi An continued to captivate Maddy with its culture and people. It was filled with restaurants and artist stalls selling everything from shrimp filled dumplings to paintings and silk jackets. Maddy browsed through scrolls of oil paintings which depicted daily life in Vietnam: rice planted by figures shown in ankle deep water bent low to tuck new plantings into the mud; doe eyed water buffalo pulling wooden plows. The quaint simplicity and appreciation for the slow processes seemed distinctly Eastern to her, and very desirable.

She sighed and remembered the conflict between her and Richard on just this topic. He wanted to buy a bigger house, to amass more things, to move forward, while she was always trying to cut back, slow down and live simply. He had labeled her a non-achiever and slowly she had begun to believe him.

238

She smiled at the canvas of the water buffalo pulling a plow, and plucked out the painting for purchase. She would keep it as a reminder of this place, this feeling. She thanked the artist and happily paid full asking price.

She and Giovanni strolled through the fish markets and textile shops where persistent vendors tried to convince Maddy to have a silk dress made. The bolts of thick fabric were displayed like a smooth rainbow. In the open produce market, Giovanni juggled mangoes and made the children laugh. A group of people attracted by his performance gathered to watch. A man approached slowly holding a staff for support and nudged forward to see the event. He looked weak and deformed by a bulbous protrusion at his neck. Giovanni glanced up in mid throw. The four mangoes dropped to the ground in a procession of thuds. Children squealed in laughter at his unintended comedy, but he had turned ghostly white.

Maddy paid the fruit vendor for the lost mangos and pulled Giovanni out of the crowd to a quiet street.

"What's wrong?" she implored. "Are you ok?"

He nodded yes but was clearly disturbed. "That man with the growth," Giovanni Shuddered. "He reminded me of when I was sick."

"When were you sick?" She asked, wondering how many stories filled his narrative.

"Last year--in India. I almost died. That's why I'm so thin," he said. Giovanni held his arms out as if showing Maddy for the first time.

"Let's get some tea." Maddy said. "You need to sit down."

Giovanni sipped on the steaming cup and recounted his story of trekking. He had started in Nepal, then crossed into northern India to Uttar Pradesh in search of warmer weather. After trekking for many weeks alone, he longed for company and a more gentle routine. He took a room in the home of a family that raised cows for the production of ghee and he even learned to milk and churn the butter. Giovanni spent hours over huge meals with the local people talking about world politics, economics and religion.

Giovanni came down with a bad stomach flu after a trip to a neighboring village where he had eaten lunch with a gracious but impoverished family. He was already thin from trekking, but the onset of diarrhea and vomiting swept away what little girth he had started to regain. The farmer's wife tried aromatic concoctions to quiet his stomach but the illness and dehydration accelerated fiercely. Weakness overtook him. A local doctor was called in and prescribed an anti-diarrheal that was no match for the bug wreaking havoc in his system. Giovanni became wasted and too weak to travel on his own. The farmer feared that Giovanni might actually die.

"The thought of dying sounded good at that time," he said. "I was so tired, I just wanted to sleep forever."

It became clear that Giovanni must get to a hospital for help. The farmer drove Giovanni to the closest rail station, administered a healthy dose of opium to paralyze his bowel and placed him, barely conscious, on the train. Bizarre dreams came and went and he woke intermittently to find himself on the floor of the train; he could barely lift his head. He calculated later that the train ride to Calcutta must have taken at least 20 hours. When the train arrived in Calcutta, Giovanni was dragged out and left on the open platform of the main station.

"My god," Maddy gulped. "I saw bodies lying on the train platform. That could have been you."

Because Mother Teresa Hospital was home to the sickest of travelers, they had men equivalent to an animal knacker, who came by the train station daily with a huge cart to pick up the bodies of the dead and dying.

"I woke up on this giant wheelbarrow-cart stacked with bodies. The man next to me was surely dead," Giovanni said. "There were flies inside his cracked mouth." He paused for a moment in remembrance.

"The man across from me had a football-sized growth on his neck--like the man in the market today." He held his hands wide to depict the size of the mass.

"While we rode on the cart, the man pointed to his face and said 'Goiter.' He shrugged like it was nothing unusual. I stared at the growth but pointed to my bum and said--dysentery." The man shrugged again. It sounded like a typical conversation about the turns of life.

"I looked over at the dead man and thought to myself--thank god I only have dysentery," Giovanni said.

Like all the other sick and delirious travelers without

help, Giovanni was taken to Mother Teresa Hospital. He was very ill for several days but remembered how he slowly gained the ability to take tiny sips of water and drag himself to the toilet. One vivid memory he held was the evening he woke to find a bottle of Thumbs Up cola at his bedside. He sipped the room temperature cola and thought it was the best taste in the world. The next night he found another bottle of soda and a piece of naan bread left for him. He tore off miniscule bites of bread and chewed slowly. The naan was cold but salty with butter and tasted like heaven to his starved palate. The food and drink stayed down and he was able to sleep a full night without vomiting. The next evening he found more bread and cola upon his return from the bathroom, but no one could tell him where it had come from. He ate more hungrily each day and tried to stay awake to learn see who was saving him with their kindness.

"That's amazing. I wonder if I was there at the same time as you." Maddy said. Giovanni looked confused. She shared her tale of Diya and Aarush. After comparing dates, she realized that they had not crossed paths, and Giovanni continued with his story.

One day after the volunteers had delivered fresh sheets, a tall rangy figure filled the doorway of the big room. He scanned the rows of cots before entering with an armful of bottles and bread. The scruffy bearded man, who looked more like a biker than a volunteer, moved among the cots and placed bottles of water at some, cola and bread at others. He walked softly so as not to wake the sleeping or near dead. Giovanni lay still until the stranger was next to his bed.

"Hey man--thank you." Giovanni said, his eyes taking in this gracious man.

"Oh, ey--ow ya feelin?" He had a stout Scottish accent and wooly hair under a blue cap.

"Do you work here?" Giovanni asked.

"Naw, just cem by when I ken." He shrugged.

Giovanni sat up. "Who are you? Do you feed everyone?"

The man sat down at the end of the bed. "I'm Garth--nice to meet ye. I cem here wen me mate got sick and couldn't believe how many sickies has no food ne any family. They looked like they might go away the crow road."

"What happened to your friend?" Giovanni asked.

Garth dropped his face. "He died--bad infection--it took too many days to get em help."

Giovani placed a hand on Garth's back and noticed his own hand was just bones covered by skin. They sat without words and looked across the mammoth room filled with bodies waiting for fate or God.

"Thank you again," Giovanni said. "You saved me."

It had taken another week for Giovanni to get strong enough to leave the hospital. He and Garth remained friends and went on to travel together in India before

Giovanni flew on to Southeast Asia. Garth stayed in Calcutta; it seemed he had been called to service.

"No wonder the sight of the man with the goiter startled you," Maddy said.

Giovanni turned to her. "I think that I might have died if Garth had not helped me. I am forever grateful to him."

The tea was cold and flecks of green leaf clung to the sides of the smooth white cup. "Where will you go from here?" Maddy asked.

He shrugged. A far-away look inhabited his face and Maddy realized he was wandering like she was.

"I don't know. Since there is more to be seen in Vietnam, would you like to stay a few more days?" He asked.

"Absolutely. I will have to make plans to head home before my money runs out, but for now, let's see whatever we can fit in." Maddy smiled and they agreed to go back to the hotel and make plans.

Giovanni met Maddy in the lobby after breakfast the next morning. Her hair was wet and she fumbled with her day pack to find a hairband. She unearthed one and scooped her hair up into a loose twist.

"Ciao Belle," Giovanni called as he hopped up from the low couch. He gave her a European two-cheeked air kiss. "Let's go."

The way to the little wharf was only a fifteen minute walk. Maddy checked her pocket for the hand written ticket. In neat black ink it read: Cham Island Day Trip. Lunch and Snakes Included. She stared and hoped that the error meant that snacks were included and not snakes. The guest house operator had suggested the trip as a nice way to see more of Vietnam. Giovanni babbled as they walked substituting Italian words in when his English ran dry. Maddy smiled inwardly at the peacefulness of traveling with Giovanni. She smiled and pointed out a woman who rode by on a bicycle with a young girl on the handle bars of the bike. The little girl waved.

Slip number six was at the far end of a row of boats and two young Vietnamese men waved as they approached.

"Good morning," one man called. His English sounded like it was being played on mandolin strings. "Come. We leave in ten minute."

Giovanni followed Maddy and ducked down two steps into the open sided cabin. Dark solid wood framed the ceiling and railing. The smooth wood formed long benches on either side with a narrow table in between. It was like a big family table but held only three people. Maddy waved and said hi. Two women sat close together on one side opposite a man. One of the women returned her greeting with a smile. She was pixyish with sandy hair, a small yellow flower tucked behind her ear.

"Hi, I'm Esme, from New Zealand," she said anticipating the next question. Maddy replied with her name and country as did Giovanni. He turned to the man and offered a hand. The man sitting at the end of the table turned slowly and looked up from his journal. His movement was one of a continuous fluid motion, as if he were made of caramel.

"Nice to meet you. My name is Beto." His face was wide and calm. A stillness embodied him. "I am from Mexico." He returned his eyes to the paper journal in front of him. Giovanni slid onto the bench next to Beto and Maddy sat opposite. The boat sputtered to life. After a brief explanation of the day trip and location of life vests, the boatman went back up top and the vessel slid out into the South China Sea.

Dark green water rippled at the bow. The motor purred toward Cham Island. It was one of eight small islands in a protected marine reserve just off the coast. A laminated pamphlet on the table described how local preservationists worked to promote both tourism and develop a sustainable fishing industry. The woman next to Esme looked out over the water. She was fair skinned and wore a fitted fuchsia beret. Esme introduced her friend. "This is Sasha, my best friend." Sasha turned. Instead of the blue eyes Maddy expected to see, Sasha had deep, dark circles beneath her eyes.

"Nice to meet you." Sasha spoke just above a whisper.

Giovanni regarded her. Without pause he asked, "Are you well?" The direct question startled Maddy but his tone had a way of sounding neither harsh nor intrusive.

246

Somehow his accent showed concern and respectful curiosity. Sasha shrugged and looked to Esme.

"We are on the trip of a lifetime," Esme said.

Sasha slid off her beret to expose a smooth, hairless head. "A short lifetime," she said. Thin fingers grazed over the concave surface.

"We are taking a few weeks between chemo to see the world," Esme explained. Sasha tried to smile but looked as if she barely had the energy. Esme took her hand and sat tall, defiant, an attempt to be strong. Giovanni replied with genuine care. "May you be well."

At a loss for words, Maddy sat silently. She watched the two young friends who clasped hands. They could not be more than twenty-five. She imagined the courage it would take to travel while fighting cancer. Not to mention the kindness of Esme to take on the responsibly of and risk of such a burden. What if Sasha had a reaction to the chemo, or died while they were traveling? Maddy was impressed by the fortitude of both women, the kindness and commitment. As the motor stirred the water, Maddy felt a sense of understanding she had not before realized; the pure act of compassion and love could be felt between these two people. This awareness struck her deeply - how it was possible to give completely of oneself out of pure love.

The water passed in ripples and continued out into the endless sea. After an hour the boat stopped at the edge of the marine reserve. Snorkeling gear was offered to all, but only Giovanni and Esme accepted. Beto shook his head.

Sasha smiled, declined and tucked her head beneath a purple sarong to nap.

"You do not want to see the fish?" Maddy asked Beto.

He shook his head. "I am on vacation from under the water." Maddy cocked her head. He spoke in slow round vowels. "I am in the water for my work, so today, I am above."

"What do you do?" Maddy asked.

"I am an illustrator."

Again she cocked her head. "Under water?"

He smiled. "Yes. There are many beautiful things to see, to draw."

"Wow," Maddy said. She had never considered where pictures of fish or ocean creatures came from, but of course someone would have to draw or at least photograph them.

"How did you become an underwater illustrator?" The career was utterly foreign to her. His face changed as if a shadow had crossed over the sun. "I'm sorry," Maddy apologized. "That is a personal question."

Beto nodded for several seconds. "The story is both happy and sad. I love my work, but it has come with a cost." He was mesmerizing to watch. One moment he was still like an oiled wooden sculpture, the next he was as fluid as a liquid. She watched him in his statue repose for another minute and almost turned away. But moments before she did, he shared his story. As he spoke, he became fully reanimated. His smooth, dark limbs awoke and provided punctuation to the story as that of a conductor.

He had been offered a contract from a London publisher to submit pictures to a famous naturalist publication. The offer came with the condition that he come to London first and pass an English proficiency exam. He had studied English in school but was nowhere near proficient. The employer, in working with many people all over the world, offered a three-month intensive English program before sitting for the exam. He had accepted the offer and left Mexico City to study.

He and his wife Lourdes had separated the year before and shared the care of their young daughter Izel. It was very difficult for him to leave her, but knew he would return immediately after completing his exam. Three weeks after his arrival in London he received an official letter stating that Lourdes had filed for divorce and sole custody; a court date was pending. Distraught at the idea of losing custody of Izel he poured himself into his studies and waited for the court date to be assigned.

Weeks wore on without news and Lourdes would not return his calls. He missed both his wife and daughter deeply and longed to conclude his studies so he could go back to Mexico. Finally a letter arrived. He tore at the envelope so violently he almost ripped the notice that read-Due in Court, 5 November.

He stared in horror at the date which coincided exactly with the date of his proficiency exam. A wail of agony consumed him and he sobbed at the idea of having to choose between his precious daughter and his dream job. Convinced that the loss of either would denude his soul, he set about a petition to change the exam date. His first request written slowly in halting English was denied flat out, so he a pressed hard into his studies until he was able to construct an articulate, persuasive appeal. The second request for change of date was granted but only by one day; he would be able to take the exam on the fourth of November. This would leave him only one day to get back to Mexico City.

Elated, he crammed with subjunctives and superlatives until he had mastered the King's English. He spoke to everyone he met, just for practice and wrote a long letter to Izel to work on verb tense and conjugation. He memorized lists of exceptions and drilled vocabulary right up to the day of the exam.

He packed one bag, dressed neatly, and arrived early for his exam. He flew through the written portion with ease and was moved on to the verbal exam administered by a proper bow-tied gentleman with a thick accent. Beto chose each response with great precision and delivered perfect grammatical prose. Finally he sat through a series of comprehension questions of which he made a few contextual errors, but overall demonstrated that he was in fact, proficient in English. He thanked the proctors and sprinted from the building.

The tube from London proper to Heathrow airport was packed, but was still better than the crowded London byways. He dodged through airport crowds only to learn that his outbound flight was delayed. Beto paced like a captured tiger until the flight boarded four hours late. He ran through travel calculations and routes until they were imbedded in his brain: Six hours to New York then six more to Mexico City; one hour for customs and another for surface travel. He would get a hotel near the courthouse to cut down on travel time, then shower and shave and dress. He would just have time to make it to the courthouse by first opening.

Beto's panic mounted as his flight out of JFK was delayed by four hours due to weather. He recalculated his travel numbers and would still have time to shower before the courthouse opened. He slept briefly on the six hour flight but woke up startled and disoriented over Mexico. The captain came on the loud speaker to announce that instead of landing at Mexico City International Airport, they would be diverted to Licenciado Aldofo Lopez Mateos International Airport in Toluca. His fingers tapped as he reset his calculations and his watch to Mexico time. If all went well he would make it to the courthouse shortly after opening.

As with travel plans in general, things did not go well. Customs, not expecting the diverted flight, was late to open and traffic between Toluca and Mexico City was worse than he had remembered; busses and cars and motor bikes jammed six lanes across and jockeyed into impossibly narrow openings. He finally arrived in the city center and found a small hotel. In minutes he showered and dressed and pressed his wrinkled shirt against his body on the way to the courthouse. He arrived by ten o'clock and inquired about the docket list for the day.

"Ese juicio ya ha sido escushada." The woman behind the window said.

"Done? Already?" he shouted in English and looked at his watch. Impossible. The courts never started on time; it couldn't be done already. He ran down the hall and stuffed coins into the payphone and prayed for Lourdes to pick up.

"Did you get her?" Maddy leaned toward Beto, realizing she was holding her breath.

Beto shook his head. "No, I lost custody of Izel and Lourdes moved back to her family's home many hours from Mexico City." With the story concluded, Beto returned to a mannequin repose. "I send a letter each month addressed to the grandparent's home in hopes of a reply."

Maddy stared at the water. She looked at Beto's sun darkened face. There were no words that worked. She felt his sadness. She knew the loss of being separated from a child. Like a small part of your heart was missing. A deep ache filled her. "What is the happy part of the story?" Maddy asked.

"I have the most amazing work. It is my passion, my dream," Beto replied. "I know one day I will see Izel again. My heart knows how much I love her." He turned back to his journal and studied the last entry. Maddy excused herself and stood on the back of the boat looking over the open ocean. Its endlessness made her feel small. She closed her eyes and let the emerging sun cover her.

Fifteen

Maddy said good bye to Giovanni the next afternoon and boarded a bus heading west. She decided to travel across Laos on her way back to Bangkok. The seven hour trip across Vietnam into Laos was a bumpy trudge past brushy scrub forest interrupted by farmland and more rice paddies. She arrived late in Vientiane, checked into a dingy guesthouse, and fell asleep directly. In the morning she woke, disoriented by yet another country. Maddy sat on the edge of the bed and cringed to see the room in the dim light. The sheets were prison grey and creased with dirt. The mattress was as thin as a saltine cracker. In the lobby, the hotel owner looked like a plum that had been left in the sun for weeks. He smiled a wrinkled grin with only four teeth.

Vientiane, the capitol of Laos, was a wide sleepy city that still preferred bicycle transport over cars. Official buildings were a colonial design and contrasted against the blocky concrete construction of the hotels. She walked the streets and looked for an open restaurant. It struck her at how quickly life could change. Just a day before she was with newly found friends. Today she woke up in a filthy room and wandered alone in search of a meal.

Green papaya salad was the first thing on the menu of the simple food cart at the end of the block. A young woman shredded green papaya into a mammoth mortar, added a glug of fish sauce, a hefty squeeze of lime, and threw in a small handful of chilies. She used a giant pestle to pound like a jackhammer; her thin wrists strained beneath latex gloves. Next, she stirred in garlic and bitty dried shrimp. Maddy took her spicy salad bowl across the street to a narrow park to sit and watch the city move.

Bicycles, as if on a carousel, rounded a huge traffic circle. A group of young monks whispered and giggled as they walked in a cluster through the park, their saffron robes flapped like wings. Maddy watched a thin amputee hobble on crutches from bench to bench. According to the guidebook, landmines continued to be a major cause of mortality and disability in Laos; a dark legacy of the American-Vietnam war.

The crisp papaya was an excellent vehicle for the garlic and chilies. Maddy's eyes watered with each savory bite. She finished off a full bottle of water and wished she had another. She strolled through the open streets and considered moving out of the prison hotel but decided to stay one more night since she had already paid, and so as not to offend the wrinkled owner. A little more dirt wouldn't kill her. She returned later in the evening to the nearly deserted hotel and was confronted by a thick, hairy ex-pat who'd just landed in Laos. He was overweight and greedily held a plate of chicken skewers and rice close to his mouth.

"Where you coming from kid?" he said to Maddy, rice escaping his lips as he spoke.

She had hoped for a quiet evening but couldn't ignore his large presence. "Oh, I'm on my way to Bangkok," she said.

He grunted and stuffed a cube of chicken in his mouth. "Girl like you shouldn't travel alone."

"Ok, thanks," she said. "I'll be careful." She scurried to her room and locked the door. Now she was in her cell with a dodgy guard and felt like a trapped animal. She looked at the cracker-thin bed with the dirty sheets and was filled with dread. Mustering some fortitude, she covered the sheet with her sarong and wrapped the pillow with a clean tee shirt. Staring up at the ceiling, Maddy realized she was tired of moving from place to place. Meeting new people was fun, but she had the urge to find her place, to hunker down for a while. A glance at her traveler's checks told her she had about one month of travel money left. Only thirty days to figure out her life. She hated the idea of returning home, returning to her old job, and dealing with Richard. The thought exhausted her and left a hollow feeling in her stomach. Maybe she would just stay abroad, find a job. But just having a job didn't feel like enough. She wanted to do something more. She fell asleep before she could sort it all out.

It was dawn when she gathered her things and left the

hotel. The city was hazy and a fog hugged the tree tops like a wool blanket. She had read that the Thai border was twenty-five kilometers from Vientiane. Maddy walked in that direction in hopes of catching a local bus. Feeling edgy, she walked fast under the weight of her pack and startled at the occasional motor bike that whizzed by. Two young men peddled silently past her, causing her to jump with a shriek. A local bus went by, then slowed and Maddy ran to the open door.

"Does this bus go to Nong Khai?" she asked. The driver nodded and she jumped aboard. It was sparsely filled with women headed to early morning jobs or crossing into Thailand to shop in a larger market. Maddy sat down, happy to be in the company of women. The bus bumped to a stop at the border and she walked over The Friendship Bridge into Thailand.

Nong Khai was more narrowly laid out than Vientiane but the people and surroundings were the same. Maddy dropped her pack, sat down on a curb, and pulled out her travel books. She knew she was dragging her feet by stopping one more place before going back to Bangkok. Somehow it felt like she needed to have a plan before arriving back there. Maddy looked at her stack of books. The poems by Rumi reminded her of Ethan. He had moved to Bangkok accidentally, and things had worked out well for him. Louisa's words came back to her: "You'll know, when you know." Maddy hoped that was true.

The guidebook offered several budget lodging choices.

One called The Guesthouse Retreat jumped out at her with the promise of daily yoga, meditation, free bicycles. She scribbled the name and address on a piece of paper and waved down a motor-taxi. The guesthouse room reminded her of Mr. David's place in Siem Reap: dark wood walls and a harem bed. This one however, was covered with pink mosquito netting. The room had an outdoor shower tiled in blue glass and mini built-in planters that made the shower walls a living garden. It was exotic and elegant, a far cry from the dirty grey sheets she had escaped that morning.

Rosie was the front office manager, the housekeeper, and the meditation instructor in one. She greeted Maddy brightly at the front desk. Rosie unfolded a map and pointed out several sites to visit.

"The Buddha Park is very nice--only a thirteen kilometer ride. It has hundreds of Buddhist and Hindu statues," Rosie said.

Maddy traced the road map with her finger. She circled the other tourist venues as Rosie spoke. As Maddy tucked a yoga schedule under her arm, she turned out the door, missed the step, and splayed onto the gravel path; paper flying into the air. Rosie ran toward her but Maddy picked herself up and brushed the spiky gravel from her chin. A trickle of blood glazed her fingers. Embarrassed, Maddy went quickly to her room. The cool shower stung the gash as she stood under the water until the blood was gone.

The next morning she woke to a swollen purple chin and hauled her sorry face off to a yoga class. Reluctant joints creaked in objection; despite her efforts to breathe, she felt leaden and worried. At noon, she signed out a bright orange bicycle and walked it toward the road. Cars and busses kicked up dust as they shuttled down the narrow highway. Maddy's hair and eyes were gritty when she pulled into Buddha Park. She spat several times to clear the dirt from her throat.

Huge stone statues loomed up from the grassy area and crowded the entrance. Buddha in every form filled the park: the pudgy Chinese depiction, the broader, more stalwart figure of a Japanese style statue. Further down the park was a mammoth reclining Buddha with its head propped in hand. Maddy walked more than one hundred paces end to end. It was like the Golden reclining Buddha at the Grand Palace, but made of stone. The stone was stained in striations as if tears of acidic rain had left coppery lines. Multi-faced statues surrounded the reclining Buddha and reminded her of the Bayone at Ankor Wat, vacant eyes that saw everything.

Maddy sat beneath a figure of Buddha meditating inside the flare of a cobra's hood with multiple smaller hissing mouths rising from the original snake head. She looked out over the hundreds of statues and considered the wisdom and traditions embodied therein. The enormity and complexity felt burdensome.

The puffy, dark gouge on her chin quivered as sadness fell over her. She was lonely, lost, and adrift. She slumped around the park for another hour before she returned to the orange bike and peddled back to the guesthouse.

Midweek, Maddy decided to ride the bike to the countryside. Just as she began to peddle, it began to rain. She considered returning to the guesthouse but she was trying to avoid sitting around worrying. Besides, she remembered a quote from an old friend back home: 'The worst weather makes for the best stories.' In that spirit, she rode on.

By mid-morning, water had pooled in the rutted roads. It sprayed off her spinning wheels and dirt covered the orange fender of the Schwinn. A car passed her so close that she felt the side mirror graze her thigh. Breathless, she edged over to the furthest part of the road before continuing on. Less than two kilometers later, as she crossed a narrow bridge, a travel bus bore down on her skinny spinning wheels. She peddled furiously to clear the bridge, but just at the far end, the spray made her wobble on the slick road. The bicycle tipped into a long, low skid and slammed her body to the pavement. The bike flew off into the ditch and disappeared among the tall roadside grass. Maddy cried out in pain as she sheared across the roadway. She came to a stop many feet from where she left her skin. Small cars zipped by without noticing her crumpled, bleeding body on the shoulder of the road. It was not until another bicyclist passed that someone stopped to help.

The man was old and small. He looked more Chinese than Thai. He didn't speak a word of English. He bent close as if nearsighted and peered down through wrinkled eyes at Maddy's bleeding limbs. His hand so soft, as to be almost imperceptible, touched her forehead and she turned tearful eyes toward him. He spoke the foreign pluck of Thai and Maddy shook her head. Ever so gently, he bent to help her up. Blood mixed with rain and ran down her legs like diluted paint. She checked her bones and found them still aligned. She could see that muscle and flesh had borne the brunt of the crash. The old man's hands supported her weight for a few steps as the loose gravel fell from her exposed mealy thigh. He guided her back to where his bicycle lay. With effort, he managed to right his bike without letting go of her. They hobbled in the mist and road spray back toward town.

The walk was excruciating in length. Maddy was thankful for the kindness of the Thai octogenarian. At one place, they were forced to jog lightly to cross the highway and Maddy, wishing for ablation of her nerve endings, cried out as her muscles were pulled into motion. The man guided her through the open market where vendors called to him in Thai and shook their heads at Maddy's pathetic state. He didn't reply, just nodded as they walked down a narrow alley. He motioned her into a doorway with a thin flight of stairs. Gingerly she climbed the stairs which opened to a small tidy apartment. She stood in the entry, soaked but no longer bleeding. He gathered a large cotton cloth, spread it over the floor, and motioned for her to sit down. Slammed by the shock, she slumped against a pillow. The old man went about making preparations like an apothecary.

He steeped chamomile into an amber tea and dabbed it onto her raw road rash. He cleaned the wound on her leg and over her ragged elbow. Finally the tea was applied to the side of her face. A salve followed the chamomile, in a slippery layer to all the red open tissue. The berry colored rash on her cheekbone complimented the purple of her chin. Maddy winced as he worked until the salve had sealed off the cruel air from her raw flesh. A cup of flowery green tea soothed her throat. She fell into a light sleep. Rushing water filled her dreams, toppled trees and mud that filled homes with its unforgiving sediment. She woke to throbbing muscles like a multitude of toothaches in her bones. The aged man sat next to her drinking tea, his lips moving as if in prayer.

Maddy fished into her daypack and found the white card containing the name and address for the Guesthouse Resort. He took the card, nodded and returned it to her. Maddy cried out when she rose from the floor. Whimpering, she realized that they would have to walk to the other side of town. Before they left the humble dwelling he handed her a small plastic bag of salve. She hugged him and they set off across town.

For the remainder of the week Maddy rested and pasted on salve. The mealy skin was beginning to scab over in some places. The rain slowed to a drizzle and Maddy got a tuk-tuk to the central market and gingerly climbed out. She walked up and down the stall rows scanning the faces of all the men. She was planning to leave the next day for Bangkok but wanted to thank the elderly man who had helped her. Back home, people would help in an emergency, but it was extraordinary that this silent stranger had taken her to his home and cared for her. She desperately wanted to thank him for his generosity.

Newly de-feathered chickens hung upside down from their feet in the stall next to the heaping piles of red and yellow chilies. Dark green leafy chard was wrapped in bundles and tied with coarse twine. She limped along at a sorry pace and stopped to rest whenever a seat was available. Thai faces blended together by the end of the isle. She ventured down some small alleyways off of the back of the market, ducking beneath hanging laundry and weaving around kids playing ball in the puddles. None of the alley's looked familiar, nor did any of the men. Dejected, Maddy realized that if she continued to wander deeper, she would be lost and require help yet again. She traced her steps back out to the market and gave up on her quest. Back at the guesthouse she paused in front of a small Buddhist statue. She added some rice to the offering bowl and gave thanks to the compassionate man by proxy. She hoped the universe would repay his kindness in full.

In Bangkok, the traffic outside the train station was thick and noisy compared to the small villages in which Maddy had spent the last month. She sighed and took in the city scape. She knew her travels were drawing to a close; money running low and the reality of a pending divorce weighed on her shoulders. She walked toward a sign indicating a bus stop and sorted through a handful of Thai coins. As she walked, Maddy was struck with the awareness that she had actually become a world traveler: She had taken a train to an unknown part of the city with no help and no production; she had flown alone several times; she had made her own plans. A feeling of accomplishment filled her. She hadn't needed Richard or anyone else to make decisions for her. In fact she was sure now that Richard had been a limitation for her, an excuse to stay stuck in her ways.

Besides the huge potted plants on the patio at the Ranee Guesthouse, the courtyard was empty. Maddy called out to see if the owner was there.

"What happened to you?" Neils asked.

Maddy touched her face realizing that she was still bruised; the cut on her chin turning to a green-yellow pallor.

"I fell, and crashed a bike." She shrugged. Maybe that was why people were giving her a wide berth on the bus. "Do you have a room available?"

"Sorry, No. We are full just now. In a few days maybe." Neils said.

"Darn. Ok. I'll check around," she said.

"Before you go, I have a message for you." He disappeared into the closet-sized office and came back with a creased piece of paper.

"Thanks," Maddy said and read the scrawling words.

Please call when you get this message- love Caroline

"When did this come?" Maddy said turning the paper over and back.

"It came on the fax machine about a month ago." Neils said.

Maddy had given Caroline the phone and fax number of the Guesthouse to use as a point of contact. "Thanks again," she said.

There were plenty of other places to stay on Kho San Road but Maddy liked the feeling of going someplace familiar. Her search led her blocks away and right to the doorstep of Ethan's books. A smile broke across his face when Maddy came in, as though she was a long lost friend.

"Welcome back!" He hugged her in a whopping embrace. Maddy laughed, then winced as the pressure of his body crunched her still healing skin.

"Well look at you." Ethan held her at arms-length. "You look like you have been in a bar fight."

"You did encourage me to go out and be notorious," Maddy replied. Somehow the bike crash sounded less exciting to her than a bar fight.

"What brings you back?" Ethan asked.

"Just wrapping up the last few weeks of travel. Running out of money. I'll be booking a flight home soon," she said.

"Brilliant. I can buy back your Vietnam / Cambodia

travel book, and maybe you can join me and my friends for a bottle or two of Singh Ha beer tonight."

"Sounds great. By chance do you have a phone that works with calling cards? I have a message from home."

"Sure. Come around to the office here." Ethan led her down a small hallway. The desk was filled with stacks of travel books. Some new, most used. Maddy sat down at the phone happy to be surrounded by books. Her hand trembled slightly as she dialed in the international relay number.

Caroline picked up on the third ring. "Hello?"

"Mom, it's me. I got your message to call. Is everything ok?" Maddy breathed deep and squared up a stack of books.

"I don't know how to tell you this. You had better sit down," Caroline said.

"I'm sitting." Maddy's stomach dropped. "Just tell me."

"Richard." Caroline paused. "He's dead." The line stretched silent between them.

Maddy's mouth opened and closed. Finally she asked, "When? How?"

"There was a flood, or a landslide. Somewhere in Sumatra. He was there at an orangutan refuge or something. The flood took out the whole village," Caroline said.

"Maybe he wasn't there," Maddy said. "How do you know he was there?"

"He had mailed a postcard in the weeks before saying he was going there. Then I got a call from his brother.

They found his body, his backpack, and his passport downstream."

"That can't be. It's impossible. We didn't have that on the map at home. We weren't going to Sumatra." Maddy said.

"You have been apart for months Maddy. He continued to travel just like you did." Caroline said. "I'm sorry to have to tell you this bad news."

Maddy stared out the door of the office. Ethan was helping a man pick out some books. "Thanks for telling me. I have to go. I'll call you back soon, I promise." She disconnected the line. Her body full of lead and disbelief.

Ethan finished up and came into the small office. He stopped short when he saw her face. "What happened?" He said.

"My husband. He's dead."

"Oh god. How did it happen?" Ethan asked.

"I guess he was in Sumatra. There was a flood in a village by an orangutan reserve." Maddy spoke the words robotically. They made no sense to her.

Ethan's face darkened. "Oh, yeah--it's been all over the news-- so sad. I may still have the newspaper report. Let me look."

He began to dig through a box stacked with old newspapers. Maddy stood on shaky legs and watched him flip papers from one pile to the next. As he searched she became weak and sank to the floor, slumped against the wall.

"I can't believe this. I left him fine and healthy a few months ago. And now he is gone." Maddy voice was a far-away drone.

The silence was measured by the turning of the newspapers. Ethan stopped and picked up a paper with an original article. He handed it to Maddy but she shook her head and said, "Will you read it to me?"

The unusually high rain volumes in Sumatra this season took their toll in the town of Bukit Luwang. Flooding was reported earlier in the week along the Bahorok River, and trapped the residents of the small town on the south side. The town is accessible only by a two mile hike and a hand ferry to cross the river, one man reported. "We tried to get people across the river but the water rose too fast."

After days of rain the hillside came down and the town, perched on its side, came along with it. The orangutan rehabilitation station gave way and it, along with all the smaller outbuildings, hotels, and restaurants were swallowed up by mud. "We could hear the orangutan in the night screeching and moving in the trees, but couldn't see anything until morning. By then, the whole town was gone."

Maddy lowered her head to the floor. The carpet was thin and worn from years of use. Ethan stopped reading and scooted over to stroke her hair.

268

The door chimed and Ethan said, "I'll be right back." Before he left he slid a stack of newspapers under Maddy's head as a makeshift pillow. Tears soaked the news print, saturating the paper. She imagined Richard's terror of being swept up in a torrent of water and mud in the dark jungle night. She imagined the cries of fleeing orangutan. These thoughts stole heat from her fingers and toes and she curled up in a fetal pose. What a horrible way to die. Guilt stabbed at her gut. When they were together she had wanted to be away from him so much that she had imagined him dead. But it was only in an abstract way, never tangible. And now he was gone. Truly gone. Had her bad thoughts caused him harm? She squeezed her eyes closed to scramble away the sad reality. Ethan returned to the office to check on Maddy who sat up when he entered. Newsprint, moistened by tears, had transferred its inky typeset onto her cheek and forehead.

"You look a mess mate. Where are you staying? I will walk you there?" Ethan said.

She shook her head. "No place. I haven't found a place yet."

"Then stay here, with me. At least until you sort things out," Ethan offered. He sounded a happy with the idea of a temporary roommate.

"Thank you," Maddy said still in shock. She accepted a key and went up the back stairs to a weensy apartment above the store. It was sparsely furnished, and generally neat, except for the stacks of books in every room. She tucked her backpack in a vacant corner and lay down using it as a pillow.

Life was strange, and short, and unpredictable. In other circumstances she might have been with Richard and would likely be dead too. A shiver rippled through her. She felt completely adrift. Aside from Caroline, she had no ties to home. The house that Richard might have kept would be sold. The job she might have gone back to felt meaningless, shallow. Maddy got out her travel journal and slowly turned the worn pages. People and places played a movie in her mind: Kathmandu; the Great Dane; saying goodbye to Chrissy as she left for the Peace Corp; Helmar and Galiana; the sweet boy who took her hand and led her to the Ganesh Gate; Diya and Aarush lying side by side on the small cot. Maddy's heart felt heavy. Where was Diya? Had she gone back for Aarush? She fell asleep on the floor with visions of Aarush in her dreams.

The next few weeks were a blur. She was glad to be busy in the bookstore to take her mind off of her worries. Instead of time slowing down for her to process Richard's death, it seemed to speed up. She spoke to each of Richard's family members in turn. It was difficult at first to explain why she had not been with him in Sumatra. As expected, Richard had not told them of their split. His sister, estranged from the rest of the family didn't even ask what happened but said: "Good lord, I don't know how you lasted so long."

Richard's brother on the other hand was eager to talk.

Roger was similar to Richard in his love for a grand story. He asked Maddy to tell him everything they had seen and done along the way. To her surprise, Maddy found the stories pouring forth. She recounted their crossing the two hundred foot suspension bridge in the Himalayas; crashing an Indian wedding with Richard stoned on a hashish smoothie; sharing a bus ride with chickens, goats and a cobra. Maddy's memories of the failing marriage were edited out for his brother. The family was in the process of getting Richard's body back to the US. It was expected to take some time so the memorial was not scheduled for several months. Maddy promised to be home by then.

"How'd it go?" Ethan asked as he closed up the shop.

"Better than expected," Maddy said. "It's so strange. Much of my life was filled with anger toward Richard, but now the positive memories have trumped all the negative ones."

"Maybe there were more good times that you allowed yourself to enjoy." Ethan offered.

Maddy swallowed hard and blurted out her fear before she could stifle it. "Do you believe that my bad thoughts about Richard contributed to his death?" She squinted her eyes to shield from the answer.

"Not unless you were doing some serious voodoo, mate. Maybe you only saw the bad things in your marriage to justify a reason for leaving."

"Or maybe there was just a lot of misery to go around," she said.

"Yeah, that's possible too." Ethan patted her back. "What's next?"

"I need to work out my money. I can't stay with you forever." She smiled and touched his shoulder in thanks. "Tomorrow I'll call my mom and see if she will help me sell the house. I definitely can't go back to it."

"Until then," Ethan said, "let's go watch a second run move with subtitles and eat some hot Thai curry." He shut out the store lights and locked the door.

"Can I ask a big favor?" Maddy sat on the bookstore office floor hoping the international connection would hold. "Will you loan me some money until the house sells? I can pay you back then."

Caroline's end of the line crackles. "Sure, that's fine. I take it you're not coming home?"

"No. I have another stop before then."

"Where?" Caroline asked.

"I have to go back to India," Maddy said.

"To do what exactly?" Caroline said.

"I don't know. I'll figure it out when I get there." Maddy hoped her mom wouldn't ask any more questions because the answers were sure to be thin. "Thanks mom. I love you."

It took a few weeks, but on a muggy morning in Bangkok Maddy picked up her passport sporting a new

Indian visa. Next, she refilled her traveler's checks and booked a ticket to Calcutta. Ethan looked up when the bell chimed on the door.

"When are you leaving?" He asked.

"In three days."

"That soon." He whistled. "Well, I'll miss your company and your help around here."

"I can't thank you enough for your help and support. I don't know what I would have done." She could feel tears of gratitude well up in her eyes.

Ethan gave her a big hug. "You can come back any time."

Maddy picked up a guide book for India. "I'm going to need this again."

Sixteen

Calcutta was just as she'd left it, crowded, dirty, and totally amazing. It was a little less overwhelming this time since she knew what to expect. Without hesitation, she drank from clay cups and ate from even the more questionable street vendors. After checking into a guesthouse with three dogs in the open lobby, Maddy sat down with her book and map. One of the mutts ambled up and lay down next to her feet. She stroked his back with her shoe. How would she go about finding Diya? She knew her home village was Kumar Khali, several hours travel north of Calcutta. She knew Diya's father was a rice exporter. Maybe that would be enough to go on. But first, Aarush.

The volunteer waved her in at the entrance to Mother Teresa Hospital. Maddy followed the hall back toward the children's ward and stopped in the doorway panting. She hadn't realized that she'd been holding her breath. Children filled the room, even more crowded than just a few months before. Face by face, Maddy looked at every child. She hoped that Aarush had not changed so much as to be unrecognizable. Her heart sank as she scanned the last row of beds. How foolish she was to think she would just walk in and find him.

"Can I help you?" The nurse wore a white, peaked habit that looked straight out of the 1960's. It framed her wise face like a picture. Thankfully her English was proficient.

"I'm looking for a boy that was here three months ago. He was dropped off by his mother."

"Was he ill or healthy?" The nurse asked.

"He was very sick at first, but got better quickly. Last time I saw him he was up and playing," Maddy said.

"He has likely been moved to the main orphanage in Agra."

"Agra?" Maddy's mouth dropped open. She had been to Agra last time to see the Taj Mahal. It was at least a full day's train travel away. "If I go there will they let me see him?" Maddy asked.

"I can phone ahead and let the sisters know you are coming." The nurse bowed her head slightly. "Of course it will help if you are planning to make a donation to support the children."

"Yes, I will," Maddy said.

"Very good then. I will let them know to expect you."

The train platform was nothing short of a circus. Unlike last time, she now understood the controlled chaos of departing and entering a train car and was prepared for the inevitable crush. When the train pulled in, Maddy watched as car by car went by filled with people. She hoped that they were getting off to make room for the new passengers. A few did but not nearly enough.

Pressed by the throngs of people, Maddy was pushed onto the train. At the door, the crush of bodies was so great she couldn't breathe for a few seconds. Once inside, it was clear that every last inch of space was taken. She would have to do like the locals and find a space no matter how small or impossible it seemed. She tried a seat in the third car but even the native riders shook their heads. The bunk cars looked like chicken houses with people perched one atop another.

In the gap before the last car Maddy took a breath of relatively fresh air and spied a row of men crouched along the outside rail of the car. There was a narrow space and she decided to go for it. She opened the door and saw the ground rushing beneath her feet. Before she could think more about it, she stepped onto the thin metal catwalk. The men moved over a few inches and Maddy squatted down using her backpack as a seat. Warm air swirled her hair with the updraft. She knew riding on the outside of the train was dangerous, but Richard would have loved it. So in his spirit, she sat back and watched the countryside go by.

Stiff, dirty and windblown, Maddy leaned against a wall in the Agra station and looked at her guidebook. A man walked by wearing a starched white shirt. He looked at her matted hair and dirt encrusted face and dropped some rupee coins at her feet. Maddy stared.

"But I'm not homeless," she uttered. Protesting was

pointless.

She had arrived in Agra near sunset. She got a room close to the station and dropped her bag inside the door. Its size and weight were taxing. If she was going to be traveling around India she needed to pare down. As she undressed to shower she caught sight of her face in the mirror and bust out laughing. Her hair was tangled as though ratted into a beehive. Silt covered her face turning it three shades darker. She could have been mistaken for a chimney sweep. She found her disposable Kodak camera and took a picture in the mirror.

In the morning light, even the pollution was beautiful. The haze over the river between the fort and the Taj looked like an antique chenille scarf. A touch of sadness caught in her chest. She had been so busy being miserable travelling with Richard that she had missed much of the beauty. By ten o'clock the fog had lifted off the city. She stood in front of a great stone building whose signage said Mother Teresa Orphanage and School.

Children's voices rose from behind the tall walls. Squawks and laugher lifted into the air. She was glad to have brought a lunch and a book as the Indian bureaucratic process took all day. She cued up to a give her story in one office. In the next she gave her donation by signing away a small stack travelers checks. Finally she was invited in by a young volunteer who had been there for a year. Elizabeth was from Switzerland and had come to India on a church mission and stayed.

"What does he look like?" Elizabeth asked as they walked down a long, cool hallway.

"Small for his age. Huge dark brown eyes and black hair," Maddy saw that Elizabeth's smile was patient. Every child who came there could fit that description.

"We have four boys who are called Aarush. We will look in on each one."

The first boy studied with a teacher who instructed the class on multiplication tables. Maddy shook her head and whispered: "too old." The next child was very young, perhaps two years old. He cuddled a stuffed tiger toy and sucked his thumb. She shook her head again. Elizabeth continued on.

"The other boys are in the same class and may be nearly the same age," Elizabeth said. Maddy followed her past several groups of children and out onto a courtyard play area. Children ran in all directions. They played with jump ropes and kicked tattered soccer balls against the wall. Boys squatted in a group around a game of marbles.

"The boy in the green striped shirt," Elizabeth pointed. "He has been here only a few weeks. The boy in the orange shorts and red shirt has been here longer, a couple of months I believe." The boys looked similar in their build and height. Their hair was trimmed above the eyes but shaggy around the ears.

"I can't tell," Maddy said. "I only knew him for a few days. Can I speak to them?"

Elizabeth found a teacher who looked perturbed at being

pulled away for some tourist. She grabbed the red-shirted Aarush and pushed him toward Elizabeth. Maddy winced at his flimsy frame under pressure. Her heart raced. What if she could not recognize him? Maybe he would know her? Elizabeth caught his hand and tried to lead him over to Maddy. He bucked and pulled in an effort to free himself.

Up close, the boy stared at Maddy with hard dark eyes.

"Hello Aarush," Maddy said gently. She tried to imagine what he had been through in the past months after his mother left. He stared at her, lips pursed drawing his cheeks in.

"Do you remember me?" Maddy asked. "I was at the hospital. You were very sick." She reached toward his hand. Aarush pulled back yanking Elizabeth's arm with him. "It's ok, I'm sorry to have interrupted your game." Maddy grabbed her disposable Kodak and snapped a picture of the face above the dirty red collar. The boy's eyes turned steel and he yanked away from Elizabeth's hold. Before he turned, he lunged forward and spat at Maddy, then tore off of rejoin the other boys.

"I'm sorry." Elizabeth shook her head. "Some of the children have trouble adjusting."

Maddy wiped the spit from her wrist. "No worries. I don't know if he knows me and doesn't like me, or doesn't know me and doesn't like me."

The teacher, holding the green shirted Aarush by the shoulder, beckoned to Elizabeth. This Aarush allowed Elizabeth to talk to him and guide him over gently. She introduced him to Maddy. Still as a statue he stood and took her in. His eyes soaking up every bit of information possible. Maddy waited, hoping for a smile or a flicker of recognition, but the boy peered out and did not speak.

"Aarush, do you remember me?" Maddy asked. "I met you in the hospital with your mother." He did not move, did not flinch. His eyes were an endless pool of dark water. Maddy took a quick picture of him and then said thank you. He looked at Elizabeth who nodded. He turned and walked back to the play area.

"It's truly remarkable how similar they look," Elizabeth said.

"But clearly they have very different demeanors." Maddy tried to recall what Aarush was like. When he was sick he was quiet and passive. The only other time she had seen him was from afar while he shared a meal with another boy. She had no idea what he was really like in day to day life.

"Maybe he would recognize his mother," Elizabeth tried.

Maddy knew that she would have to find Diya. "Thank you for your help," Maddy said.

"And thank you for your donation." Elizabeth led her to the front entrance. "Good luck. Maybe I will see you again."

Traffic clogged the streets and horns absorbed Maddy's frustration. This whole plan was stupid and foolish. What was the likelihood of her recognizing a boy she barely knew or finding a woman she had known for two days?

"Madam," called a rickshaw driver. "I can take you wherever you wish." He motioned her to the seat.

On heavy legs, she trod toward him. "I need to find a camera shop, and a place to buy a bag." She had decided it was time to dump her huge backpack and travel lighter. The driver smiled a full row of white teeth. She climbed aboard and he peddled off with bare feet. Maddy marveled at the strength of his pencil thin legs.

The scenic tour took them past the towering Taj Mahal and the Agra Fort that loomed over the dark river that ran between them. Maddy had loved the fort when she and Richard had come through Agra before. The grand walls, three stories high, jutted up above the winding moat. It was straight out of an ancient tale. She recalled the cool, cavernous courtyards stitched together by stone carved hallways.

The buzz of a passing motorcycle disrupted her reverie. Horns honked as the rickshaw took up the center of the intersection. Maddy waved at the drivers who bleated at them. She laughed. Last time she was in India she had been so overwhelmed and so focused on Richard and their problems, she had missed the best parts of being there. She had missed the hidden order behind the chaos; how everyone got through the intersection like boats crowding into a narrow harbor. She had missed the beauty of the passing saris that fluttered from the back of motorcycles. She had missed the patience of everyone when a lone cow brought everything to halt.

The driver stopped at a small doorway and pointed to her camera. Maddy popped in and came out with a slip. "It will take several hours," she said. The driver nodded. "What is your name?" Maddy asked.

"Shrikant," he replied.

"Very well, will you take me to the market?"

"Yes madam, then we will return here for your pictures."

After a fifteen minute peddle, they entered the shopping alley by the food vendors. Fruits and vegetables were laid out in heaps atop blankets on the ground; white and yellow potatoes, red chilies, and green beans piled next to bright orange carrots. The colors formed a beautiful tapestry. A row of nuts, cashews and almonds formed mounds adjacent to a bin of black cardamom seeds. Their deep earthy scent wafted out from the stall. Maddy wished she could shop for and cook the amazing food she had tasted. The thought of returning to an American grocery store held no hope.

"There." Shrikant pointed to a shop with bolts of fabric stacked on either side of the door. "They have travel cases."

She browsed through the small hard-shell suitcases and floppy duffle bags until she happened on a small green canvas rucksack. It was barely half the size of her current pack and very low tech. No fancy compression straps or compartments. She would have to ditch a great deal of gear, but it was time. She needed to travel light, to be able to get on and off a train without heaving her cumbersome load.

It will be good practice she thought, traveling light. Time to loosen her attachment and truly explore her strange new freedom. She purchased the bag and rejoined Shrikant for the trip back across town.

In the evening the temperature cooled. Light waned across the rooftop of the backpacker hotel. Tables and chairs were arranged haphazardly on the open patio. Maddy sat down with a large piece of garlic naan bread and a spicy chutney. She flipped through her pictures. The pictures of the two Aarush boys sat side by side. She studied the photos up close. The red-shirted Aarush had a wild, almost feral look in his eyes. She knew that he had only been sent to Agra recently and there were no records from where he had come. It was impossible to know his story. He could be a street kid picked up in a sweep. He could have been orphaned by parents who died. Or perhaps he was the real Aarush left in the hospital by his mother.

The boy in the green shirt stared back at her through the photo. The camera caught a small reflection of her in his iris. Maddy's elbow had created an angle bracket shadow in his eye. There was a stillness about him, an old soul. Maddy touched the photo wishing to extract the truth. Would a boy who lived on the streets in poverty and then abandoned by his mother turn inward and quiet, or outward and fierce?

She slid the photos inside her guidebook and took out the map. Locating Calcutta, her finger traveled north in search of the Gorai River. Small dots along the river depicted towns and villages with vowel-filled names. Maddy sounded out each one until she came to Kumar Khali. Her finger had left India proper and rested inside Bangladesh. The town was south of a big expanse of the Ganges, just after it split into the Gorai River tributary. The town had stuck in her mind when spoken by Diya months ago. It reminded her of a romantic movie with characters named Kumar and Kathy. She circled it on the map. It was a long shot at best but she was here, on a quest, and would follow it as far as it would go.

Seventeen

The rail stations got smaller and smaller as she clicked
north from Calcutta. Despite the size of the towns, the train
cars were always full. Traveling with a down-sized pack,
Maddy was able to find a seat and store her bag underneath.
Humidity glued her green cotton tee shirt to the vinyl
seatback. She had finally given into the reality of train
travel: long queues, no order, lots of pushing, and a slow
ride. It no longer frustrated her. She knew that eventually
she would arrive at the intended place. There was a certain
rhythm to train life. Having made peace, she enjoyed the
journey.

She got out her journal and jotted down all she could
remember about Diya; her slightly crossed teeth, the mole
by her temple, her clothes, her voice. Maddy tried to
reconstruct the day they had met. It was hard to believe
that one of the boys she had recently seen was the same
limp boy that had lain in Diya's arms. A twisting thought
occurred to Maddy. What if neither of the Aarush boys was
Diya's son? That idea saddened her. This whole fantasy of
uniting them had a high risk of ending in total failure. But
the odds didn't seem to matter. She recalled the memory

of Diya's face when she told the story of giving birth to Aarush on the side of the road. It was a look of palpable love. Maddy swallowed around a lump in her throat. She had known that love at one time; that complete sense of joy when her belly had grown round. She had dreamed of a perfect baby, pink and healthy. Grief pierced her heart and she dropped her face into her hands. The train rocked from side to side allowing Maddy to sink into the swaying rhythm. A wrinkled hand from the old woman next to her, patted Maddy's leg. It was a knowing touch from someone who had lived a long life.

This was the truth that Maddy was chasing. The reason she was traveling back and forth across India. If there was a chance to give Diya the opportunity to have her child back, to raise him and watch him grow; then Maddy would have created some balance in the universe.

The train came to a crawl on a red steel bridge in Kumar Khali. Outside the window lush green rice land stretched for miles. It was nearly dusk and the light shifted and created richer colors than during the day. The sky was pink against the brilliant green growing rice. A couple at the end of the car gathered up their belongings and got ready to disembark. Maddy grabbed her small pack and went to them.

"Hello, are you from here?" Maddy asked.

"Yes." The man said. "We live in Calcutta, but our families are here."

"I am searching for a woman I met while in Calcutta.

She is the daughter of a businessman here who exports rice. Do you know of any export companies or offices I might visit to try and find her family?"

The woman shrugged. "I would ask around at the market. Some of the rice vendors might know."

Instead of getting a ride, Maddy walked into town. The road took her past large storage bins and concrete buildings on the outskirts. Gradually the industrial area gave way to houses and the streets narrowed. She followed the roads to the center of town and then watched where people were coming from with their shopping bags. In the market Maddy scanned the face of every woman hoping to catch site of Diya's face. She quickly ruled out the women who wore red dye in their part of their hair as it was unlikely that Diya had gotten married in the past few months.

Several vendor stalls sold rice in large bags stacked four feet high. Maddy choose one and followed the narrow path between bags until she found the proprietor.

"Can I help you Madam?" The man was short and wore a long traditional tunic over cotton pants. His feet were tucked under him where he sat atop a stack of rice bags.

"Yes, I am trying to find someone I met in Calcutta," Maddy said. He nodded as if this was a routine occurrence. Maddy started to share her story but was interrupted when the man held up his finger.

"I believe we will need tea first." He disappeared and returned carrying a small tray. He poured steaming hot chai from a clay pot into earthen cups. He motioned for Maddy to have a seat on an adjacent stack of rice bags. After settling herself and accepting a cup of tea, he nodded for her to resume the story. He listened all the way through, not asking questions, not moving. His leather sandals lay quiet on the floor at the base of the rice.

The story wound down to the present. The tea cups were empty and the man's eyes were closed in contemplation or meditation. Perhaps he had fallen asleep.

"Do you have any idea where I might begin looking for her or her family?" Maddy asked. She waited for him to open his eyes. Slowly, as if coming out of a trance, he turned to her.

"Of course there is someone who knows," he said.

Expectantly Maddy leaned forward, ready for his knowledge.

"You only have to find that person who knows." The man bobbed his head as he spoke and gestured with an open palm. Maddy's hopes tumbled. He had no idea how to help her. He was only interested in company and a story. She thanked him for the tea and left. It was getting dark so she went in search of a guesthouse.

Chickens scattered when she opened the gate to the yard. The house was blocks off the main drive and was not listed in the guidebook. It was the hand-made sign that caught her attention. It read Greetings Guesthouse.

"Hello, is anyone home?" Maddy called inside the front door. A table was neatly arranged with city maps and business cards. Everything was in perfect order, which was out of order in her experience. Perhaps the place had just opened. A chicken followed Maddy over the threshold and pecked around.

"Chut, chut," said a woman who emerged from the hallway and shooed the chicken out the door. "I'm sorry. Welcome!" She said.

"Are you open for guests?" Maddy asked.

"Yes, Yes!" The woman beamed. "You are my first guest." The woman plunged forward and hugged Maddy. They nearly toppled over and fell into laughter. Regaining her balance she said, "My name is Meher. Please come. I have a very nice room for you."

Maddy followed her down the hall and out the back door. They crossed a petite courtyard full of chairs clustered about small tables. Above them a white canopy created the feeling of a private party. Just beyond, Meher opened the door to what might have been mistaken for a garage back home. The outbuilding was a converted home or storage area that now housed a block of rooms.

"The shower is there," she pointed right, "and the toilet there," pointing left. Down a short hallway were three doors each pained a different color, red, yellow and blue. Gold door frames outlined each one making it appear like a picture. Tiny designs adorned the gold frames. Crimson red painted lace flowered over the gold paint like a beautifully trimmed sari. Meher opened the red door.

The reason for the owners pride became clear. The room was small, tiny really, but fantastically decorated in ornate fabrics and stitching. Every detail was attended to. A pressed white bed cloth was overlaid with a turquoise and red fabric stitched with gold thread. A fresh pink flower floated in a paper-leaf bowl. A towel and small bar of lavender soap rested near an oval shaped mirror.

"Oh my, this is so beautiful," Maddy said. Meher hugged her again in excitement.

"Rest. Wash. Come to the patio for dinner." Meher clasped her hands over Maddy's and then left.

A single white candle sat inside a squat bowl in the center of the patio table. Still wet from the shower, Maddy ran her fingers through her brown hair. It had been months since it has been cut and had grown down past her shoulder blades. Meher peeked out from the kitchen and waved. One by one, bowls of curry, rice, creamy cucumber salad, pickled chutney and dark chapatti bread were brought to the table. The colors and aroma made her mouth water. Meher brought two small metal cups of water and plates and sat down across from Maddy.

"I am so excited to have you here as my first guest. I hope you will stay many nights."

"The food looks amazing," Maddy said. "I would love to stay. I have no idea how long I will be here."

Meher reached across the table and took Maddy's hand as though they were old friends reunited. Meher took a small amount of water from a copper bowl and sprinkled it in a circle around the plates. Then she closed her eyes and said a Hindu blessing. The pronunciation of the words was complex and beautiful. When she finished, Meher said, "Ok, now we are ready to eat." Her smile beamed across the table.

"What is your prayer?" Maddy asked between scoops of eggplant curry on smoky chapatti. There were no forks.

"It's a prayer my uncle used to give before family meals. It gives thanks for the oneness of people, food, and God."

"That's beautiful." Maddy paused. The power of that simple blessing seemed to reside in the unbounded spirit of Meher. Maddy felt honored to be present with this woman who expressed her joy so purely and without false boundaries. She had included Maddy fully into the food and ritual. Maddy felt blessed. This time Maddy reached across and squeezed Meher's hand.

"Do you have family here?" Maddy asked.

"Oh, well, yes. It is a bit complicated." Meher spoke while still chewing, and fit in bites of chutney between words. "My mother and sister live in town. They run a sewing shop, a co-op really. That is where I got all the lovely fabric." Meher jumped up and ran inside. She returned with a pile of hand-stitched napkins, shirts, purses and tapestries.

"My sister is a very talented seamstress. It started out with just the three of us, but now there are fifteen women who sew each day." Maddy envisioned a room full of women laughing and talking and sewing together.

"What about your father?" Maddy said.

Meher squished up her nose and shook her head. "He still lives in Hyderabad I think. I haven't seen him in years."

"Wow, divorce is not so common here," Maddy started to say.

"Oh no, they are still married. When my sister was fifteen my father found a rich, awful, older man and offered my sister to be his wife. My mother would not have it. She did not believe in arranged marriages and certainly not when my sister was just a child. So she moved us here, back to her family's home town."

"Wow, that's pretty bold of her," Maddy said.

Meher shrugged. "She just believes in girls and women choosing their life, not having to be only a wife."

"I'd love to meet your mother," Maddy said.

Meher's eyes danced. "Yes. Yes! We will go there tomorrow for lunch and to see the shop." She stood to clear the dishes. Maddy grabbed the cups and utensils and followed.

"I think you are supposed to be my guest." Meher laughed.

"I think we are supposed to be sisters," Maddy said. They both laughed and went off to wash the dishes together.

Bolts of fabric in every imaginable hue and texture were stacked against the walls. It looked like an open living room filled with cutting tables and sewing machines. Wooden spools of thread were stored on dowels like a forest of rainbow trees. Meher took Maddy's hand and led her past the group of women sitting on cushions stitching. Two teenage looking girls looked over a tapestry that was spread across a loom. In the next room children played some form of tag. The energy of the place was fun, peaceful, and accepting.

A stout woman stood at the stove stirring cloves into a simmering pot of milk.

"Hello, maaji," Meher said kissing her mother on the cheek. "I want to introduce you to someone."

The woman handed Meher a tray of tea. She kissed her back. "You take out the tea, then join us at the table."

The woman turned to Maddy and took both of her hands. "Hello, I am Asha. The others call me Mama Asha." Her eyes were a crisp dark brown. Crinkly lines had settled gently around her mouth as though she had smiled all her life. A powerful yet quiet feeling passed between their touching hands. Maddy felt her hopes, fears, and dreams transfer into this sage woman.

Remembering her manners Maddy introduced herself. Mama Asha carried two cups of tea to a low table surrounded by cushions covered in elaborately stitched fabric. After they had settled, Mama Asha said: "Please tell me your story."

Maddy paused. What was her story? An unlikely world traveler falling in love with India? A separated wife turned widow? A grieving woman in search of a stranger? Mama Asha waited patiently and sipped her tea. She had probably done this dozens of times with every girl or woman who crossed this threshold. Maddy could only imagine the hardships faced by the women here; the cruelty of society, culture, and family. She looked at the wrinkled but refined face and took in the depth of her compassion. Maddy took a breath and began with her story.

She shared of her fear of traveling and being away from home. She told of her departure from Richard and his later death. She spoke of meeting Diya and Aarush in Calcutta and her desire to help them. Mama Asha rocked a little and nodded as Maddy spoke. She asked a few questions about Diya and what Maddy knew of her family and history. The tea was spent and Maddy fell silent.

"I know of this woman," Mama Asha said.

Maddy's eyes flew open. "You do? Is she in Kumar Khali?"

"One of the girls told me about her years ago when she was with child. We got word of her living in Calcutta with the boy. I believe she returned home a month ago."

Maddy's mouth was suddenly dry. Could it be true that she had found Diya? "Can you tell me how find her?"

Mama Asha rose and refilled the cups and returned to the cushion. "I will send word and see if she will come. I cannot promise. She has been through so much."

A rush of relief and excitement surged through Maddy. She grasped both of Mama Asha's hands. "Thank you.

Thank you so much."

Mama Asha smiled. "You have not told me why you have come so far to help a woman you hardly know."

"I have some money that I want to give to Diya to start her life with Aarush again," Maddy said. But Mama Asha waited. She waited for the real, more personal reason. Old grief long since tucked away washed over Maddy. "I lost a child once. I was never allowed to see or hold or kiss my baby goodbye." Tears flowed down her face and were wiped away by the soft fingers of the elder woman. "When my husband died, I realized that I had some extra money," Maddy said. "That I could help Diya start a new life with her son in hopes that she would not have to live with a hole in her heart."

Soft arms enveloped Maddy in a motherly embrace. Mama Asha held her until the sorrow had passed. "It is a noble thing to help another." She held Maddy's face in her hands. "We will see if Diya will come to meet you."

Eighteen

Word went out through an incomprehensible network of vendors, washer-women, and friends in hopes of getting a message to Diya. Days passed. Maddy went every morning to the sewing co-op and stayed until dusk. She played with the children, helped make tea, and learned how to do some basic loom work. Pictures of the two Aarush boys were always tucked in her pocket in case Diya came.

On the twenty-fifth day Maddy returned to the guest house and sat in the kitchen with Meher as she cooked for four new guests. Maddy's shoulders slumped because of another day without Diya arriving.

"Please do not be sad," said Meher. "Things can take a long time, everything will work out as it should." She held out a wooden spoon covered in thick golden dahl for Maddy to taste. Meher had been busy with guests arriving every few days. Maddy did not sit on the patio with the other travelers, but preferred chopping and stirring with Meher who spoke in whispers about the accents and clothing of her guests. At night after cleaning the kitchen Maddy lay in bed and read her travel journal or the latest paperback left behind by guests who had checked out. She occasionally thought of Richard and remembered him in the early days of their relationship when they had laughed and hiked and picnicked together. She had learned that life was a mix of fate and choice. Fate seemed to fall as it would, but she could choose how she felt about it all. So she decided to remember him well. She allowed herself to grieve the baby girl she never got to know and accept that there was a chance that Diya would never come. There was a bit of sadness in that knowledge but also a quiet peace that as Meher had said, things would work out as they should.

One morning Maddy slept late and the sun was high when she woke. Meher was hanging freshly washed sheets and waved to Maddy over the line as she came out of the shower.

"Good morning," Meher called. "Can you pick up some things at the market on your way to the co-op today?" Maddy nodded, dressed quickly and collected the list. The market was her favorite assignment and she knew that Meher and Mama Asha conjured up a list every few days just to please her. Today she sought eggplant, small white potatoes, cumin, and cardamom.

The portly vendor smiled and waved at Maddy when he saw her. Fawning over his stack of vegetables, he showed her the newest crop. She bought everything on the list and added and bag of bright green peas and a block of fresh paneer cheese. She laughed as he tried to haggle with her.

On the first visit to the market she had paid a devilish ransom for a handful of vegetables. When Mama Asha learned of the price, she had marched Maddy back to the market and gave the vendor a tongue lashing. Since then, he went through the motions but only took the proper coins.

The sewing co-op door creaked open and Maddy juggled the grocery sack over the threshold. She had also picked up some dates and could not resist their sticky sweetness on the way to the shop. She was licking her date-gooey fingers on the way to the kitchen when she was met with the shy face of Diya. The vegetables fell to the floor and Maddy stared at the familiar face; the mole on her temple and the scissoring front teeth made Maddy immediately sure that this was Diya.

"I was afraid you would not come," Maddy whispered. Diya's eyes filled with tears and she lowered her eyes.

"I cannot believe you came here for me." Diya said. Mama Asha led them to the low cushions and left to fetch tea.

"How long have you been here?" Diya asked. Her fingers ran nervously along the purple thread of her robin egg sari.

"Only a few weeks," Maddy said.

"Why did you come all this way?" Diya spoke just above a whisper.

Maddy sipped her tea and wondered where to begin. "After you left Calcutta I went back to Thailand. I traveled around for a few months. I saw many amazing things but could not stop thinking about you and Aarush. Diya winced slightly at the mention of his name. She made a sound like a sob being pulled from her heart. Maddy reached for her hand. "I was about to go home when I learned that my husband had died. After the shock wore off, I realized that I didn't have to go home yet and that I had a little extra money to come back here again."

Diya looked up wiping her eyes on the loose cloth of her dress. "I didn't know what to do…" she started, but fell silent for several seconds. A stream of tears traveled down her young face. She spoke between gulps of breath. She explained that she could not face going back to the streets. She had no money to care for Aarush and he was so happy to have food and some children around. She decided to come home and find a way to tell her father. She hoped he would accept her and perhaps one day allow her to bring Aarush home.

"What did he say when you told him?" Maddy asked.

Diya shook her head. "I didn't, I couldn't. He has become so angry and stern. I cannot tell him."

They sat quiet for a minute. Maddy reached into her pocket and brought out the pictures. "I saw him," she said. "He has been moved to Agra. Actually there are two boys with the same name and I could not tell which one was your Aarush." She handed Diya both pictures to Diya. Her eyes scanned back and forth for a second and she dropped the red-shirted boy's photo. It fluttered to the floor. Her eyes took in the small green shirted boy with the dark brown eyes.

"My boy," she whispered and pressed the photo to her chest, eyes closed as if in prayer. Diya began to rock and weep, her body folded over her lap. Her thin spine poked up from under the sari fabric forming a curved ridge. Maddy stroked her hair.

"We can go see him," Maddy said to her gently. "We can go get him."

Diya's tear stained face looked at Maddy with disbelief. Her eyes reflected both hope and terror in the same moment.

"I have some extra money," Maddy said. "We can go to Agra and bring him back here. If your father will not take him, then Mama Asha will help you." Diya looked from Maddy to Mama Asha who nodded.

"But what do I have to do?" Diya's voice was laced with fear and suspicion. Mama Asha had seen this before in the women who had been promised jobs only to be prostituted or beaten.

"You will be safe traveling with Maddy. No one will hurt you." Mama Asha spoke with soft confidence. "You can talk to the women here. Many have been in your place. Now they support themselves and their children."

Diya glanced at the circle of young sewers who talked and laughed while they worked. She looked back to Maddy. "Why would you help me?"

"Many years ago I lost a baby girl. I know the grief of

being without your child. I didn't want you to live with that same sadness." Maddy spoke with ease, finally being present with her loss. Diya reached over and hugged Maddy in a tangle of light blue cloth. They sat clasped for many seconds. Maddy was not sure who needed the other more.

In the early morning haze the following week, they met at the train station. Mama Asha stayed with Diya while Meher and Maddy went to buy tickets.

"What will you do once you get the boy? Will you come back with Diya?"

Maddy shrugged. "It depends on how long it takes. I have to go home for Richard's memorial and to sort out my things, but I definitely plan to come back."

Meher brightened at this news. "You can stay with me when you return."

"I was thinking," Maddy said. "I have a friend with a small boutique shop. I think she might be able to sell the clothes made at the co-op." Maddy grabbed her small pack and put it over her shoulder. "I think I could become her international buyer." Meher hugged her and bounced on her toes.

"Thank you for helping me find Diya and for welcoming me into your family," Maddy said. "I can't wait to come back."

As Diya and Maddy boarded the train, Mama Asha took Maddy's hands in hers. "You are a good girl. Come back to us," she said.

"I promise," Maddy said and waved good bye. The conductor collected the tickets and Maddy sat down next to Diya. When the train lurched into motion Diya smiled at Maddy and took her hand as if to say thanks. Neither of them spoke. Maddy put her arm around Diya as the train picked up speed and clicked in a synchronous rhythm to the passing Indian countryside.

Acknowledgements

Deepest gratitude goes out to Christi Krug for igniting the fire of my writing, to Ken for always believing in me, to my early readers: Ann, Shirley, Debbie, Amy, Julia, and Sherry, to Tom for introducing me to world travel, and to my mother Carol, who never gives up on me and who reads, reads, and re-reads endlessly.

Special Thanks

To Coleman Barks for permission to use his beautiful translated words by Rumi, and to Bjorn Ansbro for his excellent feedback, and for helping navigate the publishing process.

CPSIA information can be obtained
at www.ICGtesting.com
Printed in the USA
FSOW04n0846020316
17595FS